DATE DUE

DEMCO 38-296

Understanding and Accommodating Physical Disabilities

UNDERSTANDING AND ACCOMMODATING PHYSICAL DISABILITIES

THE MANAGER'S DESK REFERENCE

Dorothy Stonely Shrout

QUORUM BOOKS
Westport, Connecticut • London

Library of Congress Cataloging-in-Publication Data

Shrout, Dorothy Stonely.
  Understanding and accommodating physical disabilities : the
manager's desk reference / Dorothy Stonely Shrout.
      p.   cm.
  Includes bibliographical references and index.
  ISBN 0–89930–814–7 (alk. paper)
  1. Physically handicapped—Rehabilitation. I. Title.
RM930.S47   1994
362.4—dc20   93–14120

British Library Cataloguing in Publication Data is available.

Library of Congress Catalog Card Number: 93–14120
ISBN: 0–89930–814–7

First published in 1994

Quorum Books, 88 Post Road West, Westport, CT 06881
An imprint of Greenwood Publishing Group, Inc.

Printed in the United States of America

∞™

The paper used in this book complies with the
Permanent Paper Standard issued by the National
Information Standards Organization (Z39.48–1984).

10 9 8 7 6 5 4 3 2 1

Contents

Figures and Table

Preface

The knowledge that someone we live with, work with, or play with has a disabling condition often fills us with uncertainty. How should I act? What should I do? Can I catch it? What is happening to this person? Will this person be different now? The questions are endless. Often the most difficult one is "Who can I ask?"

The physician in general practice is not expected to be well versed in special conditions and may only address the clinical aspects of an illness. Specialists are often too expensive or too busy for general consultation. Family members may be unrealistically optimistic or overly protective of a loved one.

This book is intended for people who have an interest in knowing the basic facts about a disabling condition, but who have neither the time nor energy to absorb many complicated biological concepts or bewildering medical terms. The chapters in this book provide accurate information with regard to present understanding of these conditions. This book is neither a textbook nor a technical discussion of the many disabling conditions it covers. Therefore, it requires little or no formal background in medicine and assumes no prior knowledge of the subject on the part of the reader.

It is, of course, impossible to talk about an illness, injury, or birth defect without using some medical terms. I have tried to keep these to a minimum and to explain those that are used as succinctly as possible. Some of the chapters include drawings to illustrate, very simply, the terms under discussion.

The qualifiers "may," "could," and the like are used frequently throughout this book because textbook cases of disability do not exist in real life. A particular symptom may appear in most but not all cases, or appear only rarely. The human body is capable of infinite variation.

Each chapter addresses a different condition, but it is entirely possible for one person to have more than one disabling condition. For instance, a person with diabetes may have had an amputation and may also be blind. In such cases, each condition will need to be reviewed in order to understand that particular person.

Throughout this book, I have used the full name of each condition every time it is mentioned. This was not intended to fill up space, but to help the reader accept the idea that the condition is very real. Using acronyms instead of words allows us to overlook the serious nature of those words. Using the acronym HIV allows us to forget that the "H" stands for "human." It is not, however, rude or insensitive to use the acronym in conversation with the affected person. In fact, if you find it difficult to pronounce some of the words, using an acronym is the best choice.

Finally, a few words on the organization of each chapter. The cause of each condition is identified as a birth defect, illness, or injury. Some conditions have more than one possible origin, in which case each possibility is listed. Information on treatments that may be used follows discussion of each condition. It should be recognized that treatment modalities are constantly being changed due to new information and new technologies. Some physicians are willing to use experimental treatments, while others prefer to use only time-tested methods. Therefore, treatments vary widely. Only the most widely accepted methods have been included in this book.

Acknowledgments

I wish to acknowledge my deepest gratitude to all those who helped me see this book through to completion: my children—Amy, Raymond, and Johanna—for their constant "You can do it!" attitude toward this project; my editors, Eric Valentine and Catherine Lyons, for their faith in the value of this endeavor; the staff at Planetree Health Resource Center, who could always find another source to check for information.

I also wish to express my heart-felt thanks to my friend Don, who started me on the path that led to this book. Who would have thought!

Thanks to all of you.

Introduction: You + Me + Them = US!

This informal and very subjective chapter is my way of introducing the reader to the world of interaction between people with disabilities and able-bodied people.

I have been fortunate enough to meet people with a wide range of disabilities through my scuba diving classes. Each person has contributed to my joy in life and to my understanding of the fact that everyone experiences life from a different viewpoint. Take John, for example.

John was a certified scuba diver who was also a paraplegic. He lived in a town four hours north of me and had been unable to find someone willing to dive with him. Now, it doesn't take much incentive to get me in the water, and since I was just starting to teach people with disabilities to dive, I headed north. After a brief land-based refresher on dive techniques, we hit the water. It was one of those rare days in the ocean when there wasn't much to see. Each time I managed to find something interesting on the bottom, I realized that instead of being horizontal with me, John was vertical with his head in the kelp. So I'd get him horizontal in the water and start over again. At the end of the dive, I asked John if he had seen the shrimp hiding in a crevice. He said, "Yes—but did you see me standing up?" Only then did I understand that that was exactly what I had seen—a man standing up by himself for the first time in many years!

Seeing something involves understanding what you do see. When people with disabilities look like they are having trouble doing something, it may be that they are succeeding in doing something in their own style. How do you know which is which? Ask! It is never rude to offer help. If help is needed it will be accepted. If not, don't be offended by refusal.

Then there was Leroy.

Leroy is moderately autistic. Like most people with this disability he had trouble relating to the world around him—with one exception: the ocean. Leroy was a wealth of information on marine life and Jacques Cousteau. I wasn't sure this would make it possible for him to learn to dive but I was willing to help him go as far as he could. At times it was difficult for me to judge just how much Leroy was learning in lecture. Then one night I had a minor gear failure in the pool. In a class consisting of able-bodied people as well as people with disabilities, Leroy was the only one to respond—and he did so correctly.

It's often tempting to decide how much people will be able to do based on our perception of their limits. Can you imagine living your life according to someone else's design? Allow those with disabilities the right and the opportunity to explore their own limits—then help them push those limits a little farther. How?

Ask if they think they can do this particular thing. If they say "yes," let them try. If they're unsure, allow them the opportunity to try—knowing that failure won't change their personal worth. If they tell you they can't do it, ask if they have tried before. Maybe they had all the support in the world and just couldn't accomplish the task. If so, let it be. But maybe the first time they tried they didn't have someone as creative as you to suggest an alternative method!

Christine has been "confined" to a wheelchair since an accident at fourteen left her without the use of her legs. When I met her she was a student at Stanford University Law School. Since then she has served a law internship in Costa Rica. She is married to a man who shares her love of horseback riding and scuba diving. Does this fit your definition of "confined"?

The words we use often serve to perpetuate a misconception. People "use" a wheelchair; they are not "confined" to it. The chair gives them freedom from confinement. People are victims only if they choose to be. When people have had the misfortune of a serious illness, accident, or birth defect, they are victims only if they refuse to rejoin a society that wants them. Once they have chosen to enjoy life again, give them the respect they deserve by not referring to them as victims. They are people first, last, and always.

Pam has severe cerebral palsy. She cannot care for herself and has difficulty speaking. She came to an evening scuba class not to learn to dive in the ocean, but to know what it felt like to float, to be weightless. It's my practice to challenge the limits of all students the first night in the pool. I need to know how strong they really are, how soon they tire, and how they react to stress. I asked Pam to swim four lengths of the pool. Her response was, "No problem—did you bring your breakfast?" Pam has no difficulty understanding that she has massive limitations; she knows she is "different." Even more massive than her limits is the size of her courage. She lives life to the fullest extent possible—no matter how long it takes.

Be patient. It's worth the wait. In this wonderful time of tearing down the barriers between people, don't let your preconceptions be the invisible brick wall in someone else's life. Allowing someone the opportunity to succeed is one sure way to leave a footprint in time.

Getting comfortable with disabilities sometimes takes a little help. The Windmills training program was developed by the California Governor's Committee for Employment of Disabled Persons in response to studies that found the greatest barriers to employment of disabled people are ignorance and fear. Windmills training consists of fourteen one-hour modules designed to help people examine and overcome their own irrational attitudes and biases. For information, contact Windmills, The Foundation on Employment and Disabilities, Inc., 3820 Del Amo Boulevard, Suite 304, Torrance, CA 90503 (213) 214-3430.

Another organization offering sensitivity training is Current Consulting. This group will put together a seminar tailor-made for your organization, to help employees understand and accept a co-worker with a disability. For information, contact Current Consulting, P.O. Box 112223, Campbell, CA 95011 (408) 379-6536.

LENDING A HAND

"Would you like some help with that?" It's a simple question we ask almost automatically when someone is overloaded or can't seem to get a door open. Yet if the person is in a wheelchair struggling up a curb or fighting with a door, we often don't know if it's okay to ask that courteous question. Some people with mobility impairments like to get help any time it makes things easier. Others prefer to do everything on their own. The funny thing about a mobility aid is that it doesn't change the personality of the person using it. There is as much diversity among wheelchair users as there is among feet users. So ask! But be sure you *do* ask before jumping in to help!

If your offer is accepted, there are a few things you should know about lending a hand. The first thing to know is that there is a second question you need to ask: "What would you like me to do?" The best way to do something is not always obvious, but the people you are helping are experts on their own needs. When you have completed what was asked of you, be sure people know you are leaving—they are on their own again.

If helping involves a door, hold the door and stand out of the way. Hold the door long enough for the person to get completely through to the other side.

Pushing a wheelchair isn't as easy as it may look. Begin slowly. The chair may be wider than you anticipated; you need to be sure you don't get one wheel stuck on something. The chair has foot plates that increase the length of the chair; plan for those extra inches. Don't keep running into things with someone else's feet.

If the chair becomes difficult to push, check to see if the person's foot has fallen off the foot rest. People who have lost feeling will be unaware of a foot drop and their feet may get wedged under the chair.

To get the chair up a step, there are two alternatives. One is to turn the chair around so that the back wheels are against the step; then tip the chair slightly backward and pull the back wheels up first. The second method is to place the front wheels at the edge of the step, tip the chair backward to raise the front wheels, and go up frontward. Ask the person in the chair which method he or she prefers. Always avoid tipping the chair forward, since this is hazardous and may spill the person onto the floor!

When entering an elevator always turn the chair around and back into the elevator so that you can come out facing forward.

Mobility-impaired people may be able to transfer themselves into a car or piece of furniture with little or no assistance. It is never safe to make a transfer until the brakes on the wheelchair are locked, even if you are there to hold the chair.

Carrying on a conversation while you are pushing a wheelchair is very difficult for the person in the chair. To enjoy a discussion with a person in a wheelchair, sit down so that you are at eye level. It is very uncomfortable for a seated person to look up for a long time, much less look behind and up!

People in wheelchairs will often volunteer to let you pile things in their lap while you push the chair. If the items are heavy they won't feel the weight, but it *is* going to hurt them. The increased weight reduces blood circulation in the legs. If you need to help push and are carrying something heavy, deal with both things separately.

One final tip. Electric (motorized) wheelchairs are designed to be propelled on their own and steered by the occupant. They will not go faster if you push them. They are, however, rather delicate and do break down.

When this happens the person in the chair will need help. Powered chairs are very heavy and difficult to maneuver when they are broken.

If you are going to lend assistance to a person with a vision disability or hearing impairment, there are several tips in each of those chapters that will allow you to avoid being a hindrance and truly help.

The Americans with Disabilities Act defines a disability so broadly that, at one time or another in our lives, most of us will come under its protection. When you see someone who needs help, offer it. You may need help yourself someday.

HUMAN RESOURCES AND THE AMERICANS WITH DISABILITIES ACT

Human resource professionals need to feel comfortable interviewing a person with a disability. They need to be comfortable with the condition itself, if it is obvious, and with the best method of securing good employees for their company. This book and a small amount of exposure to people with disabilities should increase the comfort level.

It is always permissible to ask an applicant "Do you think you will be able to perform the job for which you are applying with or without accommodation?" You cannot ask "Do you have any kind of disability?"

Once the job offer has been made, however, you can ask all kinds of medical questions, providing they are job-related and asked of all new employees in this job classification. If you discover a disability after the job offer has been made, you cannot withdraw the offer until the possibility of reasonable accommodation has been explored thoroughly.

The Americans with Disabilities Act (ADA) does not require employers to actively recruit people with disabilities. It was written only to assure equal opportunity to obtain employment.

If the company chooses to recruit people with disabilities, a good place to start is with a job placement service that specializes in finding jobs for people with disabilities. Most major disability organizations have job-matching services. Many companies hire by asking current employees to direct friends and family members with disabilities to their Human Resource Department.

It is very important, whether actively recruiting or not, that the people who accept employment inquiries in your company understand what they can and cannot say to an applicant who has a disability. The safest approach is to write a script for various situations and have employees practice the responses often enough that they can respond correctly but not so much that each sentence sounds like a scripted speech. The important thing for them to learn is that everyone has the right to apply for any job they choose, and the application must be accepted with the same enthusiasm for everyone.

Many employers do not have written absence policies. This oversight can be a big problem if an employer decides to terminate an employee who has a disability, based on the fact that he or she has missed too many days of work. If the policy is written and uniformly enforced, then the employer can terminate on the basis that it is enforcing its policy. If there is no policy, the terminated employee can argue that the termination was based on the disability itself, not on the fact that he or she missed too many days of work.

A worker injured on the job is not automatically covered by the ADA. But many injured workers are covered. The key is that the work-related disabling injuries must meet all the criteria that would be imposed on any disability to determine qualification under the ADA. The definition of a disability under workers compensation is different than that under the ADA, because they were written for different purposes.

Many employers are worried about excessive workers compensation costs when complying with the ADA. According to the Equal Employment Opportunity Commission, if employers follow the ADA guidelines, there should be no increase in the cost of workers compensation. ADA requirements supersede any conflicting state workers compensation laws.

Remember, a person who knowingly provides false information about his or her health during a lawful postoffer medical injury is not entitled to a job. The employer has every right to refuse to hire, or to fire, such a person.

Reasonable accommodation is necessary during the application process, which includes access to the area where interviews are being held. When setting up the interview area, the following architectural requirements should be observed:

1. The minimum clear width for single wheelchair passage is thirty-two inches at any single spot and thirty-six inches for any distance. If two wheelchairs will pass each other, the minimum width is sixty inches.
2. The space required for a wheelchair to make a 180 degree turn is sixty inches.
3. The minimum clear floor space needed to accommodate a single wheelchair is thirty inches by forty-eight inches.
4. Objects projecting from walls with their leading edges between twenty-seven inches and eighty inches above the floor should protrude no more than four inches into walkways. Objects mounted with their leading edges at or below twenty-seven inches above the finished floor may protrude any amount.

5. Protruding objects must not reduce the clear space of a wheelchair accessible route.

6. Carpet should be securely attached, have a firm pad or no pad, and have a level surface. The maximum pile thickness should be one-half inch.

7. The least possible slope should be used for any ramp. The maximum slope of a ramp should be 1:12.

8. Ramps should have a level landing at the bottom and top of each ramp and each ramp level in a series of ramps. The maximum rise for any single ramp should be no more than thirty inches.

ACCOMMODATION

What does it really mean? How far should I go? What if it doesn't work? The questions are endless and they are valid.

According to the Americans with Disabilities Act, a reasonable accommodation is "a modification or adjustment to a job or the work environment that will enable a qualified individual with a disability to perform the essential functions of a job." Notice that is says "modification or adjustment"; it doesn't say "tear down and rebuild" or "buy the most technologically advanced item on the market."

The obligation to provide reasonable accommodation to workers depends on the facts presented in each case. There is no set formula that can be applied to each disability that will yield the appropriate accommodation. The employer and employee need to spend time in a give-and-take, problem-solving session. Each needs to understand what is actually needed. The employee may not know enough about the job site operations or the work environment to make requests. The employer may not know enough about the person's limitations to suggest accommodation.

An employer is only required to provide an accommodation that specifically assists a person to perform the job. If an accommodation assists the person throughout daily activities both on and off the job, it is considered to be a "personal" accommodation and the employer is not required to provide it. However, a personal accommodation, owned by the employee, can be used on the job with no responsibility for reimbursement on the part of the employer.

In order to determine the best accommodation for all concerned, the following approach is suggested:

1. Make sure the worker is qualified. This can include such things as experience, education, license, or certification requirements.

2. Determine the essential functions of the job, not just what the job appears to be. The best way to do this is to ask someone who does the job (or knows the job) to list each task that comprises the job, estimate how often each task is done, describe how the tasks are performed, list what tools are used, state how much time is allotted to each task, determine if the pace can be changed, and decide what determines good job performance. Now determine the essential functions of the job and the ancillary tasks.

3. Talk with the person who has a disability to find out the exact job-related limitation caused by the disability. Find out how he or she thinks these limitations can be overcome with a reasonable accommodation. Don't assume technology will provide the solution in all cases. Evaluate alternatives such as altering the job or job sharing.

4. Work with the person to find possible accommodations and evalute whether they will work in your facility. Keep in mind the individual abilities, not limitations, of the disabled person and that equipment recommended for one person may not be suitable in the case at hand.

5. Use outside sources for technical assistance if necessary, but don't turn the responsibility over to them. Be sure they aim to modify the task before turning to assistive technology. The best solution is often the simplest and least expensive.

6. Look for matches and mismatches between job tasks and the capabilities of the employee. There may be an able-bodied employee who loves to do the task that the person with a disability can't do. That same person may have responsibilities he or she hates. Trade!!

7. Select and implement the most reasonable accommodation. If there is more than one option, allow the individual to make the final choice. An individual with a disability does not have to accept an unwanted accommodation. However, if the person rejects an appropriate accommodation necessary to essential functions of the job, and as a result of that rejection, cannot perform the job, the individual will not be considered a qualified individual with a disability. The employer can then offer the job to someone else.

8. Document all steps in the process of attempting to accommodate an individual with a disability—the successes as well as the failures.

Making the Workplace Accessible

Accessibility in the workplace means more than ramps, wide doors, and accessible workstations. All facilities used by employees must be accessible to employees with disabilities. This means all safety protection or procedures must take disabilities into account (check the fire alarm system!). Access to break rooms, vending machines, and cafeteria areas should be checked (if it's self-service, how will a person who is blind manage?). Training opportunities, seminars, and conferences must be open to all and should be scheduled in an accessible area. How will the person access the first aid kits or material in stock rooms? Are company activities that are held off-site accessible?

With adaptive aids and training, most people with physical disabilities can use a computer. Work produced on a computer is uniform regardless of how the computer is operated. Adaptive computer devices can make things relatively equal between an able-bodied person and a person with mobility impairment.

Mobility Impairment

AbleOffice system solves many of the problems the mobility-impaired worker has in managing files, papers, books, and other materials that are part of office work. Extensions for Independence designs workstations for people with high level spinal cord injuries. They also make a device that enables a mouthstick user to use any mouse on any computer. Lipstick, by McIntyre Systems, is a joystick mounted on a gooseneck. Moving the stick by mouth causes the pointer on the screen to move in the same direction. HeadMaster by Prentke-Romich is a headset with a sip-and-puff switch and a sensor box. Turning the head moves the pointer around the screen. When the pointer is on the letter or action desired, a puff on the switch makes the choice. Freeboard by Pointer Systems is a keyboard emulator that provides easy access to IBM-compatible computers. Dragon Systems makes a program that allows a person to run a computer completely by voice. Pilot Luggage has a Wheelchair Briefcase, which attaches to a wheelchair and allows the person to activate the chair.

Hearing Impairments

Harris Communications offers a catalog with a variety of products for the hearing-impaired, including TDDs (telecommunication devices for the deaf), telephone ring and doorbell signalers, closed-caption decoders, and alarm clocks. Edwards' Phone Page activates a remote audible or visual signal, such as a horn or light, when the phone rings. Silent Call Personal Alert monitors up to five devices and alerts that a signal has been transmitted with a vibration.

Communication

Prentke-Romich manufactures a product for nonspeaking persons that talks for them. The device communicates rapidly and accurately using a speech chip and a special keyboard. The Canon Communicator M is a lightweight communication aid for nonoral, motor-impaired persons.

Visual Impairments

Henter-Joyce offers JAWS (Job Access with Speech), a software for visually impaired people. Computability provides computer access with a video-to-speech processor. IBM offers the Screen Reader, designed to enable visually impaired people to hear the words on the screen.

This list, lengthy as it is, is only a small sample of the devices available to people with disabilities that will help them perform effectively and competitively in the workplace.

For help with accessibility issues or technical problems, consult the following organizations:

The Job Accommodation Network (JAN)
809 Allen Hall
West Virginia University
P.O. Box 6122
Morgantown, WV 26507-9984
(800) 526-7234

RESNA
1101 Connecticut Avenue, NW, Suite 700
Washington, DC 22036
(202) 857-1199

Architectural & Transportation Barriers
1111 18th Street, NW, Suite 501
Washington, DC 20036-3894
(202) 653-7834

American National Standards Institute
11 West 42nd Street, Thirteenth Floor
New York, NY 10036
(212) 642-4900

Clearinghouse on Computer Accommodation
GSA Central Office
18th and F Streets, NW, Room 1213
Washington, DC 20405

IBM Special Needs Referral Center
P.O. Box 2150
Atlanta, GA 30301-2150

ANATOMY

The human body has five levels of structural organization that are interrelated in many ways.

The first level of organization is the chemical level, which consists of all the chemical substances essential for maintaining life. These chemicals are structured to form the next level of organization, which is the cellular level. A cell is the basic structural and functional unit of an organism. There are many different kinds of cells in the human body—muscle cells, nerve cells, blood cells, and so on—each with a different structure and each performing a different task.

The next level of organization is the tissue level. Tissues are groups of similarly specialized cells, united to perform certain unique functions.

In many areas of the body, different kinds of tissues are joined together to form a more complicated level of organization, which is the organ. Organs are structures with a recognizable shape and are composed of at least two different tissues. Some of the more familiar organs are the heart, brain, liver, lungs, and stomach, each of which has at least two kinds of tissue working together to accomplish a common goal.

The highest level of structural organization is the system. A system consists of an association of organs that have a common function. For instance, the digestive system involves eleven organs—beginning with the mouth and ending at the rectum—in the processing of the food we eat.

All the parts of the body functioning with one another constitute the total organism: one human being. The key words are "functioning with one another" because a failure in one system affects at least one other system. Therefore, it's important to have at least a general understanding of the major systems of the body, the purpose of each system, and how a system failure or weakness will impact the rest of the body. It is not realistic to list every kind of failure or all of the possible impacts in this short discussion; therefore, those listed will serve as examples only.

Integumentary System—consists of the skin, hair, nails, sweat glands, and oil glands. Its purpose is to protect the body, regulate body temperature, eliminate wastes, and receive certain stimuli such as temperature, pain, and pressure. If the skin is badly burned, it cannot protect the body from infection, nor can it contain the heat needed to keep the chemical reactions of the body functioning.

Skeletal System—consists of all the bones, their associated cartilage, and the joints. Its purpose is to support and protect the body, give leverage, produce blood cells, and store minerals. A broken bone in the neck can be a fatal injury. Bones that do not produce enough blood cells impair the body's ability to move oxygen through the blood and to maintain heat.

Muscular System—includes all the muscles of the body. Its purpose is to help bring about movement, maintain posture, and produce heat. A failure of the muscle of the heart can cause death. Skeletal muscles that weaken can interfere with walking, cause bone deformity, and reduce the body's ability to maintain warmth.

Nervous System—consists of the brain, spinal cord, nerves, and sense organs such as the eyes and ears. Its purpose is to regulate the body's activities through nerve impulses. If the brain is injured, the processes that are controlled by the injured area are stopped. If the spinal cord is severed, all function controlled by nerves at and below the break in every system will be affected.

Endocrine System—includes all glands that produce hormones. Its purpose is to regulate the body's activities through hormones carried in the blood. A failure in the pituitary gland affects the growth of long bone. A failure in the ovaries or testes affects the ability to reproduce.

Cardiovascular System—includes the heart, blood, and blood vessels. Its purpose is to distribute oxygen and nutrients to the cells, carry carbon dioxide and waste from the cells, maintain the acid/base balance of the body, protect against disease, help regulate body temperature, and prevent hemorrhage by forming blood clots. A failure in this system can cause cells to die, the body to become poisoned by wastes, or fatal bleeding.

Lymphatic System—consists of lymph fluid, lymph vessels, lymph nodes, and glands such as the spleen, thymus, and tonsils. Its purpose is to filter the blood, produce blood cells, protect against disease, and return proteins to the cardiovascular system. A failure in this system can cause hemorrhage or allow disease-causing organisms to invade other parts of the body.

Respiratory System—consists of the lungs and a series of passages leading into and out of the lungs. Its purpose is to supply oxygen to the cells, eliminate carbon dioxide, and help regulate the acid/base balance of the body. A failure in this system can cause illness and death.

Digestive System—consists basically of a long tube and its associated organs such as the mouth, salivary glands, liver, gallbladder, and pancreas. Its purpose is to perform the physical and chemical breakdown of food for use by cells and to eliminate solid waste. A failure in this system can result in starvation or poisoning of the other body systems.

Urinary System—consists of organs that produce, collect, and eliminate urine. Its purpose is to regulate the chemical composition of blood, regulate fluid and electrolyte balance and volume, help maintain the acid/base balance of the body, and eliminate waste. A failure in this system can alter the blood's ability to do its work and can cause the body to poison itself.

Reproductive System—consists of organs that produce the reproductive cells and the organs that transport and store reproductive cells. Its purpose is to reproduce the organism. A failure of this system has the least—and greatest—effect. Other body systems are not affected by the inability to reproduce. However, reproductive cells that are abnormal can cause defects in following generations. Additionally, complete failure of this system in all members of a family brings an end to that family.

A very important physiological feature of the body is its ability to maintain homeostasis. Homeostasis is the condition in which the body's internal environment remains relatively stable, within certain limits. Every body structure, from the cell to the system, contributes in some way to keeping the internal environment within normal limits. When the internal environment is either above or below its limits for any appreciable length of time, the systems begin to shut down and the person dies. Fortunately, the body has many regulating devices that can bring the internal environment back into balance. This feature is particularly important for people who have a serious illness or traumatic injury.

The human body is at once extremely fragile and incredibly strong. Our fascination with it has kept scientists enthralled for generations and will continue to do so for many generations to come.

Physical Disabilities

ACQUIRED IMMUNE DEFICIENCY SYNDROME

Classification: Illness

AIDS stands for acquired immune deficiency syndrome. It is an illness that damages a person's ability to fight off disease; therefore, the body is unable to defend against a wide range of common and uncommon infections and malignancies. AIDS is not a single disease, but rather a collection of diseases caused by an underlying viral infection.

The history of acquired immune deficiency syndrome in the United States is relatively short. In 1981 doctors in Los Angeles and New York reported unusual cases of Kaposi's sarcoma and a rare pneumonia to the Centers for Disease Control (CDC). The CDC started to track the growing number of these reports and in 1982 began to refer to the condition as acquired immune deficiency syndrome. There is some evidence that the disease has been in the United States for a much longer time but was previously unrecognized.

More than two hundred thousand people in the United States have been diagnosed with acquired immune deficiency syndrome. The condition affects all ethnic, cultural, and age groups. There are more men with the illness than women and more women than children. At present there are thirty thousand children who have the virus that causes acquired immune deficiency syndrome.

A person does not suddenly get acquired immune deficiency syndrome. It is the result of the following chain of events:

Exposure to human immunodeficiency virus (HIV)

Infection by human immunodeficiency virus

Incubation period

Active illness (the person has "AIDS")

Exposure to human immunodeficiency virus is the first step on the way to acquired immune deficiency syndrome, but does not necessarily mean that it will certainly develop. Human immunodeficiency virus is a very fragile organism. It is easily killed by heat, ordinary soap and water, household bleach, alcohol, and the chlorine in swimming pools. Scientists at the CDC have found that when body fluid that contains the virus dries, 90 to 99 percent of the virus in the fluid is disabled (unable to infect). The virus cannot penetrate undamaged skin. For these reasons you cannot get acquired immune deficiency syndrome by shaking hands with or having lunch with a person who has the condition.

EFFECT ON LIFESTYLE

No other disease has generated as much fear and rejection as has acquired immune deficiency syndrome. People with this condition suffer not only from its effects but also from being isolated and alone. Even when there is no outward sign of illness, people who acknowledge having the virus find it difficult to maintain relationships with family and friends; find and keep jobs; pursue educational goals; join clubs; or get medical and dental treatment.

APPEARANCE

People with AIDS are more prone to infections because their immune systems are weakened by the virus. This causes an overall "sickly" appearance. In addition, weight loss associated with the disease will cause extreme thinness in some people. When the virus infects the brain, memory lapses will be a troubling problem. Periods of extreme exhaustion are common to people with acquired immune deficiency syndrome, as is depression.

ACCOMMODATION

The Public Health Service (PHS) says: "AIDS is a blood-borne, sexually transmitted disease that is not spread by casual contact. . . . No known risk of transmission to co-workers . . . in offices, schools, factories, or construction sites. . . . Workers known to be infected with (HIV) should not be restricted from work solely based on this finding. Moreover they should not be restricted from using telephones, office equipment, toilets, showers, eating facilities, or water fountains."

For those whose concern is food service, personal service, or health care the PHS says: "All laboratory and epidemiological evidence indicates that blood-borne and sexually transmitted infections are not transmitted during the preparation or serving of food or beverages and no instances of (HIV) transmission have been documented in this setting."

Since blood is often present during medical and dental procedures and is a source of transmission of the disease, the PHS has outlined recommended hygiene measures to prevent transmitting HIV in a health care setting. In addition, the Bloodborne Pathogens Standard written by the Occupational Safety and Health Administration has become law and must be followed by all the occupations it encompasses.

Section 504 of the U.S. Federal Rehabilitation Act of 1973 and the Americans with Disabilities Act of 1990 protect the employment rights of people who are infected with human immunodeficiency virus or who have acquired immune deficiency syndrome.

In addition to accommodation required by law, a company or other organization may choose to grant a more flexible schedule, reduced schedule, or modified job responsibilities to a person with active illness. Insurance coverage is an important benefit that can be structured to accommodate specific needs. The most important accommodation, however, is education for those with whom the person with acquired immune deficiency syndrome will come in contact.

RESOURCE

National AIDS Information Hotline
(800) 342-AIDS

AMPUTATIONS

Classification: Birth Defect, Injury, or Illness

Amputations are sometimes performed following damage to a limb caused by a major injury or illness (diabetes, frost bite, malignant bone tumor, etc.). There are, however, many children born with all or part of a limb missing.

There are approximately 311,000 amputees in the United States. At the present time, 7 percent are under twenty-one years of age, 58 percent are between twenty-one and sixty-five, and 35 percent are over sixty-five.

When a limb is surgically removed, the remaining portion is properly called the stump. It can take several months for the stump to mature or stabilize. Until then the diameter at the severed end is subject to shrinkage. Tumors of the nerve tissue, called neuromas, form at the cut ends of some major nerves. These neuromas emit constant impulses, which may be the cause of "phantom limb" sensations. Many amputees experience the presence of the missing limb. The experience varies from benign to extremely painful.

Limbs missing at birth are known as congenital amputations or limb deficiencies. Most of these conditions have an unknown cause. There are two types of congenital amputations: dysmelia (the entire limb is missing) and phocomelia (the middle segment of the limb is missing). In phocomelia, the child is born with the hand or foot attached directly to the shoulder or hip and it is often removed in early infancy. Absence of the outer bone in the lower leg (the fibula) combined with a deformed foot is a common condition.

TREATMENT

Amputation causes a considerable change in the symmetry of the body which, in turn, affects posture and body image.

If the amputation was surgical, the stump will be bandaged during the healing process. Swelling will be controlled by use of a compression sock that applies gentle but even pressure to the stump.

When a prosthesis is to be used, the person will be measured and fitted for the most suitable device and rehabilitation will begin. If the amputee is a child, the process of fitting a new device will continue intermittently until maturity.

EFFECT ON LIFESTYLE

The effect that amputation has on a person's lifestyle depends on several factors, including whether one or two limbs are missing; how much of the limb remains; when the amputation occurred; and whether or not a prosthesis is used. Usually the net effect is not on what an amputee can do as much as on how it is done.

Absence of one upper limb can only be partly compensated for by a prosthesis. Most people will use the intact upper limb to the maximum and the prosthetic limb only as an occasional helper. Usually, above-the-elbow amputations are less functional than below-the-elbow ones, even with a prosthesis. Some people with upper limb amputations high in the arm or at the shoulder feel that the prosthesis is in the way and choose not to use it. Absence of both upper limbs, whether partial or total, is another matter. Obviously the prosthetic arms become very important for these people. Often children born without arms become very adept at using their feet and toes as a compensatory method.

Single above- or below-the-knee amputees walk quite well with a prosthesis and, once the psychological adjustment is made, are very minimally disabled. Double lower limb amputees can walk, sometimes with the aid of canes or crutches, if there is some remaining stump that allows the attachment of a prosthesis. Double lower limb amputees can find walking for long periods very tiring and may choose to use a wheelchair on occasion. If the amputation is at the hip, a wheelchair is usually required at all times.

APPEARANCE

If prostheses are used, lower limb amputees have an appearance no different from able-bodied people. The only indication of missing lower limbs would be in gait while walking or running and climbing stairs. Single lower limb amputees are taught to lead with the sound limb when ascending the stairs and to lead with the prosthesis in an extended position while descending. Bilateral above-the-knee amputees sometimes need a crutch or railing in order to climb stairs. Typically they climb and descend stairs in a sideward manner. If no prosthesis is used, the person will appear entirely normal except for the absence of a limb or limbs.

People with upper limb amputations are usually more easily identified simply because the limb is within our usual field of vision as well as the fact that they may choose to use a hook type rather than a hand type prosthesis.

A single upper limb amputee can be thrown off balance quite easily when carrying weight with the sound limb. This is because the prosthetic arm may not compensate in accordance with the principle of opposition. Balance can often be regained by exaggerated leaning away from the weighted side.

Persons with both limbs missing at the shoulder have serious balance problems. The balance centers in our ears tell us when we are out of balance; our arms then make the necessary correction. For this reason, many people without upper limbs choose to use wheelchairs. People without upper limbs often become very adept at using their feet and toes in place of hands and may not wear shoes for this reason. Some people will use their mouth to supplement use of the feet.

ACCOMMODATION

Little accommodation is needed for the person who has a lower limb amputation but is ambulatory. One thing that can cause a problem is rough, uneven surfaces. Take a walk along anticipated travel areas and look for such things as mats or area rugs with up-turned edges, small or sudden changes in grade—anything that might present a tripping hazard. If a wheelchair is needed to supplement walking, standard modification will be necessary. The person with a missing upper limb may need to have workspace arranged to facilitate the use of the sound limb. People with both upper limbs missing will need to have individualized workspace suitable to their needs.

RESOURCE

The National Foundation/March of Dimes
1275 Mamaroneck Avenue
White Plains, NY 10605

AMYOTROPHIC LATERAL SCLEROSIS

Classification: Illness

Amyotrophic lateral sclerosis (ALS) is a progressive motor neuron disease that attacks the body's muscles and nerves. There are no recorded cases of anyone "catching" amyotrophic lateral sclerosis, although its cause is unknown. It is usually fatal.

Nearly five thousand people in the United States develop this condition each year, and this number is expected to increase. Amyotrophic lateral sclerosis is considered a disease of the middle years; the average age at the time of diagnosis is about fifty-six years old. With the aging of the population, the number of new cases is expected to increase steadily. Fifty percent of people with amyotrophic lateral sclerosis live three years or more after diagnosis. Twenty percent live five years or more, and up to ten percent will survive more than ten years.

Amyotrophic lateral sclerosis (also known as Lou Gehrig's disease) affects the nerve cells that control the muscles we move voluntarily. For some as-yet-unknown reason, nerve cells in the brain and spinal cord (motor neurons) slowly degenerate, causing the muscles they control to weaken and waste away. People with this condition eventually become physically disabled. They may also have difficulty speaking and swallowing and may be prone to infections. Pneumonia is a common illness for people with advanced amyotrophic lateral sclerosis.

Motor neurons are among the largest of all the nerve cells in the body. They reach from the brain to the spinal cord and from the spinal cord to the muscles they control throughout the body. When the motor neurons die, as happens in this condition, the ability of the brain to initiate and control movement of the muscle dies along with them.

When a healthy person wants to pick up a pencil, the brain sends electrical and chemical "messages" to nerves designed to instruct the hand to move.

Motor neurons pick up these messages and provide a pathway for them to travel along to the hand. After the motor neuron has carried the message to the end of its pathway, it releases the message to the hand muscles. The muscles then understand and respond by picking up the pencil.

Messages are carried to the body's muscles through two types of motor nerve cells. Upper motor neurons, which receive their signal from the brain, begin in the brain and send their nerve fibers downward in the spinal cord. Lower motor neurons are located in the front of the spinal cord and send their fibers outward to arm and leg muscles. As motor neurons deteriorate in amyotrophic lateral sclerosis, firm scar tissue forms in the areas where degeneration occurs and there is no way for the impulse to detour around the blockade.

Amyotrophic lateral sclerosis causes the individual motor neuron to die so it cannot receive or transport the vital message to the muscles. Electrical and chemical messages originating in the brain never reach the muscles to activate them. Muscles that are never stimulated or used become weak and eventually useless.

Interestingly, not all motor neurons are damaged in this condition. The cranial nerve that controls movement of the eye muscles almost always remains untouched. Most people with amyotrophic lateral sclerosis maintain control of their bowel and bladder functions.

Although the disease paralyzes the voluntary muscles, a person with amyotrophic lateral sclerosis remains alert and able to think clearly. All five senses are virtually unaffected.

Amyotrophic lateral sclerosis occurs in three different forms, depending on which motor neurons are affected.

Bulbar amyotrophic lateral sclerosis results from the loss of motor neurons at the stem of the brain. Muscles that control speech, swallowing, and breathing are located in this area and are eventually rendered useless.

Primary lateral sclerosis, involving the upper motor neurons, results from the loss of motor neurons that extend from the brain through the spinal cord. The first indications of disease in this area are muscle weakness, spasticity, and exaggerated reflexes.

Progressive muscular atrophy involves the lower motor neurons and results from the loss of motor neurons that originate in the spinal cord. The first indications of disease in this area are muscle weakness and wasting in the arms or legs and loss of reflexes.

Regardless of where amyotrophic lateral sclerosis begins, the disease eventually affects almost all muscles under the person's voluntary control. Nerve and muscle destruction is usually well underway before most people are aware of having a problem.

TREATMENT

There are several experimental drugs now being tested in the hope that they can stop the death of the motor neurons. However, the major success so far has come with improved ability to control the symptoms of the disease. Doctors can prescribe medications to relieve muscle cramping, ease spasticity, and control involuntary muscle twitching. Modern technology assists those who have difficulty breathing.

EFFECT ON LIFESTYLE

Because the disease progresses at different rates in different people, it is impossible to say how rapidly any individual will become disabled. As voluntary muscles deteriorate, patients can still see, feel, hear, taste, smell, and think. Many people continue their normal activities for a relatively long period of time.

Eventually, muscles that control speech will fail and weakened limbs will require the use of walkers and wheelchairs. In the late stages of the disease, some people have difficulty breathing and may need to have a breathing tube inserted in the windpipe.

Although amyotrophic lateral sclerosis robs the body of strength and control, the loss is slow and the mind remains intact throughout the course of the disease. This often causes feelings of discouragement, anxiety, and discontent. There is no pain associated with amyotrophic lateral sclerosis.

APPEARANCE

In the early stages of amyotrophic lateral sclerosis, there will be muscle cramping, twitching, and spasticity. Eventually a wheelchair will be necessary for transportation, and in the final stages of the disease the person will be bedridden.

When there is difficulty with swallowing, excess saliva will accumulate causing drooling. Tube feeding will become necessary.

Muscles that assist in breathing eventually fail. A plastic tube can be inserted in the patient's windpipe through an opening in the neck to allow easier breathing. This procedure is called a tracheostomy. When further breathing assistance is needed, a respirator will be used to artificially inflate the patient's lungs.

ACCOMMODATION

People with amyotrophic lateral sclerosis need to talk about their feelings of fear and anxiety, and feel relief when they do. Most are afraid they will lose close friends if they express their fears. Sympathetic friends, family, and co-workers can help the person to cope.

Any disease that limits the ability to speak removes an important link to the world. High-technology devices have been developed to help these people communicate, thereby decreasing the feelings of helplessness and enabling them to have a more meaningful life.

The disease places a heavy burden on the family of a person with amyotrophic lateral sclerosis. There are serious impacts on social and financial stability when a family is caring for a person in the final stages of the illness.

RESOURCES

ALS Society of America
15300 Ventura Boulevard, Suite #315
Sherman Oaks, CA 91403
(818) 990-2151

National ALS Foundation, Inc.
185 Madison Avenue
New York, NY 10016
(212) 679-4016

Muscular Dystrophy Association, Inc.
810 Seventh Avenue
New York, NY 10019
(212) 586-0808

ARTHRITIS

Classification: Illness
Over one hundred different types of arthritis have been identified, but most people who are affected have either osteoarthritis or rheumatoid arthritis. Since these two forms of the condition are the most prevalent but quite different, they will be discussed separately.

Osteoarthritis

Osteoarthritis is thought to affect over 40 million Americans—16 million severely enough that they need medical attention. This form of arthritis is a degenerative joint disease that occurs when cartilage in the joints becomes thin and begins to crack. Not only is this disease found worldwide, but it occurs in all animals that have a bony skeleton, including birds, amphibians, reptiles, and mammals.

All joints in the body have at least two interrelated bones. The tip of each bone in the joint is covered with cartilage, which allows it to move without actually rubbing against the other bones. Cartilage does not have a blood supply so it must receive nourishment from another source to remain healthy. The entire joint is encased in a thin membrane (the synovium), which produces a thick fluid (synovial fluid). This fluid allows the cartilage to absorb nourishment as it lubricates the joint. Cartilage absorbs its nourishment by acting like a sponge during periods of exercise. If joints do not get exercised, the cartilage does not get fed and eventually atrophies, leaving the ends of the bones unprotected and free to rub against each other. As a result, the joints become inflamed and stiff.

Age at onset and the rate of disease progression vary widely from person to person. In the early stage of the disease process the pain and stiffness tend to come and go. Eventually constant pain discourages use of the joint, ultimately leading to joint failure and disability.

Osteoarthritis is not due to aging alone, but is also caused by abuse of a particular joint. People who perform repetitive activities on a routine basis are prone to develop arthritis in the stressed joint, especially if that activity involves impact or weight on the joint.

TREATMENT

Diagnosing the kind of arthritis present is the first step to proper treatment. Proper treatment, however, will vary from patient to patient and from physician to physician. The common goal in all cases is to reduce pain and maintain joint function.

Pain-reducing techniques include drugs (asprin, asprin-like substances, steroids, etc.); heat applied in various ways; and arthroscopic surgery to flush out debris from bone and cartilage that may be causing the pain.

Maintaining joint function can include everything from reducing joint workload (shedding pounds or using labor-saving devices), to regular low-impact exercise, to replacing the diseased joint with an artificial one made of metal and plastic.

With the ever-increasing range of treatments available, people with arthritis can often lead normal and productive lives, with a minimum of pain and functional loss. If the treatment being used isn't giving relief, there are other options that should be explored.

EFFECT ON LIFESTYLE

Changes in the weather can cause an increase in arthritic symptoms in most people. Changes in barometric pressure, changes in termperature, and rainy weather have all been shown to increase the pain of arthritis.

Many people with osteoarthritis find it difficult to dress themselves or to cook a meal. For some a lifelong and beloved hobby is no longer possible.

If the condition is causing hip or knee deterioration, it may be difficult for the affected person to conduct everyday life with ease. Getting up from a chair, climbing stairs, driving a car, or walking can be painful if not impossible.

ACCOMMODATION

Labor-saving devices for the hands may include everything from voice-activated computers to Velcro fasteners on clothing. Anything that will reduce the need to bend the fingers will be of value.

If walking has become a problem, a motorized scooter is usually the vehicle of choice. This device has a single front wheel and two wheels in the back, and appears larger than a wheelchair. The fact that it is not a wheelchair gives a very important psychological boost.

Rheumatoid Arthritis

Nearly 5 million Americans (three times more women than men) have rheumatoid arthritis—a systemic, inflammatory, autoimmune disease. Children with the condition, called juvenile rheumatoid arthritis, account for thirty thousand of those affected. The average age of a child at diagnosis is six years old, with many cases occurring as early as two years old.

There are many differences between the disease in adults and the disease in children. The most important is that between 60 and 70 percent of the children will be free of active disease after a period of about ten years. Only 20 percent of adults have permanent remissions.

In rheumatoid arthritis, the synovial tissue surrounding the joints produces too much fluid. This causes the joints to become swollen and unstable, making movement limited and very painful. It most commonly affects the hands, wrists, knees, and feet; then the elbows, shoulders, hips, and ankles. Juvenile rheumatoid arthritis also affects the neck vertebrae. In severe cases, the joints will become deformed and internal organs such as the heart, liver, spleen, and lymph glands can be adversely affected. The juvenile form has an associated chronic eye inflammation that can lead to blindness if not treated promptly. Treatment for the eyes is usually easy and successful if begun early.

TREATMENT

Treatment for mild cases of rheumatoid arthritis is much the same as for osteoarthritis. However, there are several powerful drugs that are used for severe cases. These drugs slow down or stop the basic mechanism of the disease by targeting the immune and inflammatory systems. They can take several weeks or months to show their effects. One of these drugs is an antimalarial drug that works to improve joint mobility. Another is gold salts, which are very helpful in reducing inflammation. The anticancer drug, methotrexate, has been quite effective in some people. Corticosteroids are potent anti-inflammatory drugs that are used in the most serious cases and only when other drugs have failed. All of these drugs have moderate to serious side effects and must be carefully monitored by a physician.

EFFECT ON LIFESTYLE

During the active phase of the disease the effect of rheumatoid arthritis is much the same as for osteoarthritis—with one exception: the pain of osteoarthritis occurs when the joint is utilized, while the pain of rheumatoid arthritis is constant and intense.

APPEARANCE

Affected joints will be swollen, hot, red, and painful to the touch, have limited motion, and make sounds when they are moved, and there will be loss of muscle strength. Joint deformity may be evident.

ACCOMMODATION

One of the simplest accommodations is to allow the ambulatory person extra time to get from here to there. A lunch time schedule that begins earlier than usual will reduce the possibility of being bumped in a crowded cafeteria.

Implements and accessories that are useful to a person who has upper body paralysis will be useful to a person who has rheumatoid arthritis in the hand, wrist, elbow, or shoulder.

If the person uses a wheelchair, it will most likely be a motorized chair, and accommodations for it will have to be made.

RESOURCE

The Arthritis Foundation
1212 Avenue of the Americas
New York, NY 10036

ARTHROGRYPOSIS
(Arthrogryposis multiplex congenita)

Classification: Birth Defect

Approximately five hundred children are born every year with arthrogryposis, a congenital disease characterized by inflexible joints and weak muscles. The condition is obvious at birth. This is not a hereditary condition, although its exact cause remains unknown.

Arthrogryposis is characterized by limbs that are fixed in almost any position, due to a dominance of fatty and connective tissue in the joints in place of normal muscle tissue. Some or all joints may be involved. In spite of the awkwardness of joint positions, there is no pain associated with this condition. This birth defect varies tremendously in its effect, with some children in wheelchairs and others only slightly affected. The intellect is not involved.

TREATMENT

Early treatment often leads to some improvement in mobility but the child will never be cured. Surgical treatment combined with casts and braces is the usual medical approach. Physical therapy can increase the range of motion somewhat if done early and consistently.

EFFECT ON LIFESTYLE

The person with arthrogryposis may or may not be able to walk. If the hands are involved to a large extent, activities such as eating, writing, and dressing will be restricted.

There are some associated conditions that may affect people with this condition. These include congenital heart disease, urinary tract abnormalities, respiratory problems, abdominal hernias, and some facial abnormalities.

Until fairly recently, many children with this condition were kept at home in an attempt to protect them from injury and persecution from other children. As our society opens up, adults and children with arthrogryposis will be more evident.

APPEARANCE

The person with severe arthrogryposis has some or all of the following abnormalities:

Shoulders that are turned in

Elbows that are extended with no elbow creases

Forearms that are turned palm down

Wrists that are flexed and turned inward

Fingers that are curled into the palms

Hips that are bent upward and turned outward

Knees that are either bent or straight

Feet that are turned in and down

Limbs that may be small in circumference

Joints that appear larger than normal and have loss of motion

Spine that may show curvature

ACCOMMODATION

The major need is to accommodate a restricted range of motion. If the condition affects primarily the shoulders and arms, a person may need to work standing up in order to utilize arms that don't bend. When writing is a problem, voice-controlled devices can be used. If the person uses a walker, be sure there is plenty of time to get from place to place.

RESOURCE

March of Dimes
1275 Mamaroneck Avenue
White Plains, NY 10605

ASTHMA

Classification: Illness

Bronchial asthma is among the most common chronic diseases known. Nearly 16 million Americans suffer from bronchial asthma. Statistics in other countries are equally high. Asthma is often thought to be a benign disease, but approximately four thousand people die from asthma in America each year.

Asthma is not a problem with getting air into the lungs, but a problem with getting it out! During a normal inhalation, a person lowers the diaphragm and swings the ribs out; the lungs get bigger so that air moves from the nose or mouth through the trachea, bronchi, and bronchioles into the alveoli in the lungs. If there is an obstruction in the airway, the air slides around the obstruction when the airway expands. A person with asthma has no problem inhaling air. However, exhaling is a passive act. To breathe out, the healthy person just stops breathing in. The person with asthma has trouble at this point. The instant the ribs relax and the diaphragm slides up, the obstructed airways block the airflow and air can't get out. The result is a lot of air trapped in the lungs and a feeling of suffocation.

The four things that cause asthmatics to have trouble breathing out are secretion of excess mucus, swelling in the airway, muscle spasm, and inflammation in the airway from a buildup of white blood cells in the walls of the airways.

In the healthy person the airway is empty and slick. It is lined with tiny hairs that move the mucus along the surface so that it is covered with an even layer of moist, thin mucus. Beneath the mucus is a very thin membrane, almost devoid of cells. Beneath that there is a thin layer of muscle surrounded by the glands that secrete about one tablespoon of mucus per day.

When a person has an asthma attack, the airway contains not only an excessive amount of very sticky mucus, but also a lot of other body debris. Some of the cells that should be lining the airway lift off and settle in clumps in the airway. When these cells lift off, the airway becomes very easily irritated because it has lost its protective covering. The airway then attempts to protect itself from irritants by constricting. At this point the asthmatic will begin to wheeze.

The membrane below this layer, which has very few cells in its normal condition, becomes filled with white blood cells that attempt to fight off the irritants. Blood vessels that are usually small become dilated as they carry the white blood cells. The muscle layer containing these blood vessels thickens and muscle contractions begin. As the muscles contract, the mucus glands become enlarged and secrete mucus that fills up the airway. Now the person with asthma will have difficulty exhaling.

Asthma is caused by a number of things, including allergy, infections, industrial chemicals, drug reactions, and exercise.

Allergy is the number one cause of asthma. Fifty percent of people over thirty who have asthma have allergy-related asthma; for those between ten and thirty the rate is nearly 70 percent. When bactreria or viruses enter the body, the body manufactures a protein called an antibody to fight the invader. People who have allergies manufacture a unique antibody that is directed to fight ordinarily harmless things like dust, pollen, or food. So when these things enter the body it defends itself in what is known as an allergic reaction. For some people this reaction causes sneezing, watery eyes, or a rash; for others it causes asthma.

Infections can also cause asthma. This type of asthma generally originates in childhood as the result of a viral respiratory infection.

Anyone who inhales chemical fumes can develop bronchial irritation; this can be either an acute reaction or a chronic problem. As many as 15 percent of asthmatics develop the condition in response to industrial exposure. Chemicals added to foods to preserve them or enhance their appeal are frequently the cause of asthmatic reaction.

Hyperventilation during exercise is a potent stimulator of asthma. Hyperventilation cools the normally warm airways; a reflex reaction to this cooling causes asthma.

TREATMENT

There are three general types of treatment in use for people with asthma: avoidance, drugs, and immunotherapy.

Avoidance is the least expensive and easiest way to manage asthma if the causative agent has been identified. All that is required is eliminating the irritant from the person's environment. This is most easily accomplished if there is only one irritant (or very few irritants) such as the family cat or a feather pillow. Such things as pollen or dust are more difficult to avoid.

There are four approaches to drug treatment, each of which is effective in the right setting. The first approach involves using a preventive medication that is inhaled directly into the lungs on a regular basis to stop the onset of symptoms. It works by preventing the body's response to irritants or allergens. The second approach is a bronchodilator, which works by relaxing the bronchial muscles and stopping the response to the irritant or allergen. Adrenalin-type medications are the third approach and are a type of bronchodilator used primarily in emergency situations. The last option is corticosteroids, used when asthma cannot be controlled by any of the other approaches.

Immunotherapy can be used when an allergen has been identified but cannot be removed from the environment. This therapy involves injecting small amounts of the allergen into the body to create resistance to the allergen. The amount of allergen injected is increased over time in the hope that the patient's resistance will become strong enough to eliminate the asthma symptoms altogether.

EFFECT ON LIFESTYLE

Asthma is one of few diseases that can affect where and how a person lives. Weather conditions aggravate asthma problems for a number of people, but the type of weather varies from person to person. Usually, however, damp weather, humid weather, and cold weather are the worst.

Air pollution is another major cause of asthma. Automobile exhaust fumes, factory fumes, and general metropolitan smog drive many people with asthma to find another area in which to live.

Asthmatics are encouraged to exercise even if they have exercise-induced asthma, as there are effective medications that prevent most attacks. Wearing a surgical mask while exercising enables a person to rebreathe humidified air and thus lessen the risk of asthma symptoms. Swimming is probably the best exercise because the person inhales very moist air, thereby slowing down the cooling of the airway.

Asthma can develop because of pregnancy about one percent of the time. Many women with asthma get pregnant and have normal deliveries and normal children. Fortunately asthma medications now in use do not have any bad effects on the unborn baby. The key to a successful pregnancy is to keep the asthma controlled. Uncontrolled asthma causes a decrease in the oxygen content of the mother's blood, and therefore the baby's blood is also low in oxygen. This can lead to impaired fetal growth and development and can threaten the fetus' very survival.

Intense emotions can trigger asthma. That does not mean asthma is psychological; it means that stress can cause an attack. The asthmatic should regulate his or her life so it is as free from emotional strain and anxiety as possible.

One of the most overlooked effects that asthma has on lifestyle is economic. The estimated cost of treatment for asthma patients in the United States in 1990 was nearly $6.2 billion. This figure includes lost work and school time, as well as hospitalization and medication costs.

APPEARANCE

The appearance of a person with asthma is absolutely normal until an attack strikes. Then he or she will wheeze and begin to fight for breath. If panic sets in, the person's eyes will be wide with fright. The face may be puffy and red, and he or she will be agitated. After a particularly bad bout the person will be tired.

ACCOMMODATION

This handicapping condition can immobilize a person even though the nerves and muscles work. Asthmatics may be unable to stand because of the effort required just to breath. Some people may use a motorized scooter to get around. Conversation is difficult because they often don't have enough strength to finish a sentence.

It is important to remember that during an attack, the asthmatic person feels that nothing is as important as getting that next breath.

If an attack occurs in the workplace, allow the person time to take medication. If the medication is not effective he or she will need to leave. When the attack is severe, someone should take the person home.

If the cause of asthma is an allergen in the work environment, a face mask that will filter the air may be necessary. When that is not effective, reassignment to another position is an alternative.

RESOURCES

American Lung Association
1740 Broadway
New York, NY 10019

Asthma and Allergy Foundation of America
1717 Massachusetts Avenue, NW, Suite 305
Washington, DC 20036

AUTISM

Classification: Birth Defect

There are between two thousand and four thousand children born with autism each year in the United States. It is a biological disorder of unknown cause that affects boys four times more often than girls. Autism is not the result of poor parenting, but an abnormality of the brain itself or a defect in the body chemistry that affects the brain. In fact, the root cause may be different for different children.

Children born with autism have a nonprogressive developmental disability with a unique triad of abnormalities: communication, socialization, and behavior.

Symptoms of autism can appear in infancy or early childhood and the severity of the condition appears related to the child's age at onset. Autism that is observed very early (infantile autism), with persistent abnormal patterns of development, is generally more severe. Childhood-onset autism is diagnosed after apparently normal development until the second or third year of life, followed by regression in communication and the onset of characteristic behavioral symptoms.

The diagnosis of autism is not made on the basis of a single symptom but rather several symptoms. There are sixteen behavior patterns frequently seen in children with autism: distaste for cuddling, lack of eye contact, resistance to change in routine, difficulty interacting with peers, gesturing to show needs, no fear of real dangers, acting as if deaf, standoffish manner, resistance to learning, marked physical overactivity, inappropriate attachment to objects, sustained odd play, inappropriate laughing and giggling, spinning of objects, hand flapping or rocking, sparse meaningless speech or echo speech. When a child has several of these behavior patterns, the diagnosis is usually autism.

TREATMENT

At present, there is no cure for autism. Both the autistic symptoms and the overall outlook for autistic people and their families can be improved by psychoeducational and behavioral therapies. Persons who are mildly affected are likely to be highly responsive to early and intensive therapy.

EFFECT ON LIFESTYLE

The impact of this condition can be divided into two categories: relating to other people and learning of all kinds. Autistic people will need lifelong help relating to others and will need a great deal of help in making and keeping friends. Getting and keeping a job is a constant challenge.

Whether or not autistic people are retarded is a subject of much debate. It is possible that the child has normal mentality but lacks the communication skills needed to express intelligence. However, the practical fact is that 75 percent of autistic children function and test as if retarded.

Some autistic people have special abilities in areas like music, art, or numbers. Often these talents are quite remarkable. When they are present the person is called a savant (French for "one who knows"). Less than one autistic child in ten has these special abilities.

An unusually high number of children with autism, 20 to 40 percent, will develop seizures similar to those seen with epilepsy and will need anticonvulsant treatment.

People with autism have normal life spans, which means that autism is not confined to childhood but is seen at all ages. Given appropriate treatment, most can be successfully integrated into the community.

APPEARANCE

Autistic people are of normal size and appearance with none of the abnormal facial and body characteristics often associated with mental retardation. However, the autistic person will have an obvious emotional distance from peers, will prefer an isolated existence, and will be overly compulsive in routine.

ACCOMMODATION

Persons with autism should be taught appropriate functional and academic skills in age-appropriate community settings. Clear physical arrangement of the work environment, predictable group and individual settings, and clearly defined activities enable these people to use their visual and spatial strengths to overcome communication and social deficits. If the work environment is to be remodeled or even repainted, the autistic person will need to be informed and thoroughly prepared for this change. No physical accommodations will be needed.

RESOURCE

The National Society for Children and Adults with Autism
1234 Massachusetts Avenue, NW, Suite 1017
Washington, DC 20005
(202) 783-0125

BURNS

Classification: Injury

Approximately three hundred thousand Americans receive disfiguring injuries from fire every year. Another sixty thousand people are involved in a chemical accident that results in serious burns. In the early 1980s very few people who were burned on 70 percent or more of their body survived that devastating injury. Today more than half of them will survive.

People who initially survive severe burns undergo extensive and prolonged physiological changes. A severe burn elicits a response from the body that involves almost every organ system; the skin, nerves, circulatory system, pulmonary and kidney function, and immune system are all affected. Many thermal injuries result in amputations. In addition to the effect on the body, psychological and social needs are impacted.

Burns are classified as superficial, partial-thickness, and full-thickness depending on how deep the burn penetrates the body.

Superficial burns are first-degree burns. First-degree burns, which include sunburn, are red and painful and may have mild swelling. They affect only the outer layer of the skin (epidermis), often peel, and usually heal in three to five days.

Partial-thickness or second-degree burns damage the outer and second layer (dermis) of the skin. These burns cause the skin to have a mottled red and white appearance, produce painful blisters, and are prone to infection. The skin hair does not pull out easily and sensation is intact. These burns usually heal in two to three weeks, with possible scarring. Second-degree burns often need medical treatment.

Full-thickness or third-degree burns destroy the epidermis and dermis and extend into the subcutaneous fat, muscle, and bone. The skin may appear charred or leathery and may be black or dead white. Any blisters that formed were burned away. There is very little pain in the early stages of a third-degree burn because most of the nerve endings have been destroyed. However, within a very short time the person experiences searing pain in the exposed nerves. A third-degree burn that is larger than one inch usually will not heal without contractures that will be deforming unless treated with skin grafting. Third-degree burns always require medical attention.

A burn is considered more critical if it affects a larger area of the body. For example, a second-degree burn over 15 percent of an adult's body is considered a minor burn. If that same burn involves 25 percent of the body, the burn is considered moderate. If it covers more than 25 percent of the body it is considered critical. Any burn on the hands, feet, genitals, eyes, or face that is greater than first-degree needs medical attention.

Smoke inhalation often complicates the problems a burn victim faces. Inhaling smoke and other irritants causes an inflammatory response in the airways, often resulting in pulmonary edema and pneumonia. The patient often dies of complications when the exchange of gas is no longer possible. This inhalation injury complex is the most common cause of death in burn patients.

TREATMENT

Survival for the burn patient depends on the rapid closure of the wound after removal of the burned tissue. Typically, the dead, burned tissue is surgically removed around the fourth day after the injury. Yet the physiological changes caused by the injury do not begin to reverse until the wound is closed. Until then, the person remains defenseless against infection and draws on his or her own tissues for nutritional needs. If the wound does not close, people with burns that cover more than 80 percent of the body seem to run out of metabolic fuel after about two to three months.

Nothing is better than the person's own skin to cover the wound. Therefore, if possible, unburned skin is transplanted to the burned area—often more than once. The area that was "harvested" for the graft takes about two weeks to heal (longer with each succeeding harvest).

During this period of recovery and treatment, inhaled nitrous oxide, intravenous narcotics, and sedatives are used liberally for pain relief.

The period of hospitalization for a severe burn is very long, extremely painful, and expensive. But the problems do not end at discharge. There is usually some degree of deformity with a severe burn, even with current plastic surgery techniques. The most significant long-term problems are physical appearance and the reactions of others.

EFFECT ON LIFESTYLE

Scar tissue is an inevitable outcome of severe burns. Thick scar tissue forms contractures across joints, limits range of motion, causes scoliosis of the spine, and shortens underlying muscles.

Raised scars (called hypertrophic scars) are often red and inelastic and can limit movement. They usually appear a few weeks after healing and may continue to grow for two years or more. They are most severe on children and dark-skinned people.

Many people also lose fingers, toes, ears, or limbs to severe burns. Several years of rehabilitation are required for seriously burned people.

Physical pain is only one of many personal challenges that burn patients must confront. Psychological factors are critical for burn patients. Children have been known to describe themselves as monsters. Adults who are disfigured often don't fare much better.

APPEARANCE

If the face is involved the person may not have hair, eyebrows, or eyelashes, and scar tissue will cover the burned area.

Because scar tissue is a major concern, several methods are employed in an attempt to reduce its growth. An elastic support, called a jobst, may be prescribed as a means of reducing scar hypertrophy. The purpose of the jobst is to apply constant pressure to the healed areas, and it is made to fit the burned area like a second skin. It is worn twenty-four hours a day and, depending on the location of the burn, may be clearly visible. If the burn is on the face, the jobst will look like a mask and will cover the entire face.

Splints or braces may be added to the jobst in areas where the jobst does not conform to body contours (such as the junction of the nose and cheek). Splints are also commonly used on the hands. When these devices are used, they may be needed for twelve to eighteen months.

ACCOMMODATION

Accommodation will vary depending on the location and extent of the burn, the nature of scarring, and whether or not amputation was necessary. If amputation is a factor, treat that condition the same as any other amputation. If range of motion is limited, the work area will need to be adjusted to fit the person's ability.

The most important accommodation is a personal one. People who are extremely scarred feel ugly. It is very important to get past physical appearance and accept them for who they are. If the face has been badly burned and it is difficult to look at, try looking into the person's eyes. The person lives inside the skin and the eyes are your ticket in.

RESOURCE

National Rehabilitation Association
1522 K Street, NW
Washington, DC 20004

CANCER

Classification: Illness

In 1987 (the most recent year for which complete statistics are available) there were over two million recorded deaths in the United States. Just over 22 percent of those deaths were caused by cancer. Cancer is the second leading cause of death in both adults and children (accidents rank first for children).

However, cancer is not always fatal. It is entirely possible to be cured of cancer or to live many years with cancer depending on where in the body it is located. Nearly 90 percent of the deaths from cancer involve people over fifty-five; the average age at which cancer is diagnosed is sixty-five.

First of all, it's important to understand what a tumor is and the difference between a benign tumor and a malignant tumor. A tumor is simply the uncontrolled growth of cells in a specific location in or on the body. A common wart is a good example of a tumor. Benign tumors never spread to other parts of the body. Warts form on the skin and while they may appear on the skin of your index finger and then on your thumb, your skin is one body part. You will never find warts spreading to your liver or appearing on the lining of a blood vessel.

Normal body cells respect the limits of their role in your life. Fingernail cells reproduce and grow only at the end of your fingers. You will never find a fingernail on the tip of your nose.

Malignant tumors are formed by the uncontrolled growth of cells that have developed the ability to spread to any body part they choose. It is this characteristic that causes illness.

Warts grow on the surface of the skin. If they developed the ability to invade the layers beneath the surface, they would push the healthy cells out of the way until your skin eventually lost its ability to function as skin. When a malignant tumor grows on the surface of a lung, it eventually invades the lung itself, thereby interfering with the lung's ability to exchange gases. As healthy lung cells become more and more displaced by cancerous cells, the lung loses its ability to function as a lung.

At the same time the cancer is replacing healthy lung tissue it can send individual cancer cells into the bloodstream to be deposited in many different areas of the body. New cancers will begin to grow in these previously healthy organs; this process is called metastasis. There is no limit to the number of times or sites where these secondary growths can occur.

Any cell type in the body can become cancerous. When a cancer is discovered it is identified according to the type of cell from which it originated. Epithelial cells line all the surfaces of the body and are the top layer of your skin. When cancerous epithelial cells are identified anywhere in the body, they are called carcinomas. The correct term is therefore carcinoma of the stomach or carcinoma of the lung. Cancers of the support structure of the body (bones, muscles, ligaments, nerves, and fat, for example) are called sarcomas. Therefore, bone cancer is called osteosarcoma ("osteo" means bone) and cancer of the fat cells is called liposarcoma. Cancers of the white blood cells are called leukemias. Cancers of the lymphocytes (part of the body's second circulatory system, the lymphatic system) are called lymphomas. These four types of cancer account for approximately 95 percent of all cancers.

Cancer often does not produce symptoms until the disease is quite advanced. When symptoms do present themselves, they will be related to the function of the body part that is involved. Lumps should always be investigated.

TREATMENT

There are three treatment methods that are widely used in cancer therapy: surgery, chemotherapy, and radiation therapy. Surgery is used to remove a tumor when it can be isolated and accessed. Chemotherapy and radiation treatments are designed to reduce the size of a tumor when surgery is not an option and to kill the cancer cells if possible.

EFFECT ON LIFESTYLE

The effect of cancer on a person's lifestyle is both physiological and psychological and will depend on the location of the cancer and the chosen treatment.

Physiological effects include everything from a small scar because a minor skin cancer was removed to shortness of breath from a cancer located in the lung to loss of a limb because treatment included amputation.

Psychological effects can include depression if the diagnosis is perceived to be a death sentence, anger if the treatment leaves the person feeling mutilated, or a renewed joy in life that comes from heightened awareness of life's fragility. The effect of the illness on each individual will be as unique as the individual.

APPEARANCE

The presence of cancer will do little to affect how a person looks. Treatment of the disease is another matter. Treatment with radiation therapy or chemotherapy often makes people feel very weak and tired because of the effect these treatments have on the bone marrow. The bone marrow is where all blood cells are made. Radiation or chemotherapy treatments interfere with the marrow's ability to replace dying blood cells and results in fatigue and an increased susceptibility to infection.

The normal process of replacing cells in the body is impaired in other ways also. The growth of cells in the hair follicles is affected, resulting in a loss of hair. Intestinal problems like nausea, vomiting, and diarrhea are caused by the body's inability to replace cells in the intestines.

The cumulative effect is that the person will look and feel tired, weight loss will be apparent, and hair will thin perhaps to the point of baldness. When the treatment stops, the effects will resolve themselves.

ACCOMMODATION

The need for support from family, friends, co-workers, and employers cannot be overemphasized. A diagnosis of cancer generates fear that can translate into a wide range of reactions, including short temper, withdrawal, loss of interest, and frequent tears.

Once the course of treatment has begun, the person may need extended time off from work to recover from surgery, or perhaps flexible work schedules or reduced work loads during other treatments.

Other accommodations will depend on the location of the cancer and the results of the treatment. For instance, if a person has lost an eye to cancer, peripheral vision on the involved side will be nil, and people should be sure to stand and walk on the person's "good" side. Otherwise, the person will be able to function in the same environment as before. If both eyes have been lost, the person is now blind and accommodations for blindness will be necessary.

If there is a missing limb due to osteoscarcoma, accommodations will have to be based on which limb it is and if the person has chosen to use a prosthesis.

Surgery may have removed a cancer and left no residual effect other than the need to take a daily pill!

Take your cue from those involved. If they need to talk, then listen. If they want to forget it, then don't keep reminding them. If they need help to return to productive employment, then ask how you can help.

RESOURCES

American Cancer Society
Cancer Response System
1-800-ACS-2345

National Cancer Foundation
1180 Avenue of the Americas
New York, NY 10036

Reach to Recovery (for breast cancer)
American Cancer Society
19 West 56th Street
New York, NY 10019

American Lung Association (lung cancer)
1740 Broadway
New York, NY 10019

Canadian Cancer Society
130 Bloor Street West, Suite 101
Toronto, Ontario M5S2V7
Canada

Imperial Cancer Research Fund
P.O. Box 124, Lincoln's Inn Fields
London WC2A 3PX
England

CARPAL TUNNEL SYNDROME

Classification: Injury

Carpal tunnel syndrome is a progressively disabling and painful condition of the hand. Because the musculoskeletal strain from repeatedly flexing the wrist or applying arm-wrist-finger force does not cause observable injuries, it often takes months or years for people to detect damage.

An estimated one hundred thousand people each year undergo surgery for this painful condition, and another 20 percent of the working population is at risk of developing carpal tunnel syndrome.

The carpal tunnel receives its name from the eight bones in the wrist (carpals) and the transcarpal ligament, which together form a tunnel-like structure. This tunnel is filled with tendons that control finger movement. It also provides a pathway for the median nerve to reach sensory cells in the hand (see Figure 1). Any time the median nerve in the wrist is compressed it results in sensory and motor dysfunctions in the hand.

In the mid-1960s researchers began to observe an association between wrist disorders and the performance of certain repetitive manual tasks. A study by the National Institute of Occupational Safety and Health indicates that job tasks involving highly repetitive manual acts or that necessitate

Figure 1
Cross-Section of the Wrist

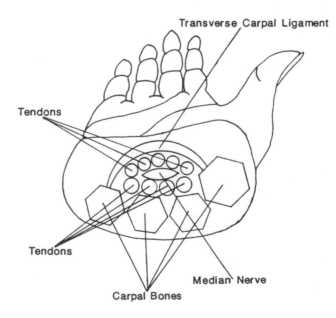

wrist bending or other stressful wrist postures are connected with incidents of carpal tunnel syndrome or related problems. This hazard is not confined to a single industry or job but occurs in many occupations.

Regardless of whether the cause is occupationally based or arises from nonoccupational sources, it has been established that repetitive flexing and extending of the wrist causes the tendons to swell and increase pressure in the bony tunnel. This, in turn, can trap or pinch the median nerve. Blockage of this nerve can cause loss of touch in certain surface areas of the hand and produce numbness, pain, and tingling in the thumb, index, and ring fingers. When this condition is detected, it is labeled carpal tunnel syndrome.

The presence of diabetes, hypothyroidism, dialysis, acute trauma, congenital defects, wrist size, pregnancy, or the use of oral contraceptives may predispose a person to the likelihood of developing carpal tunnel syndrome.

Carpal tunnel syndrome is only one of the class of injuries known as repetitive motion disorders (RMI) or cumulative trauma disorders (CTD), which occur because a joint is moved and stressed in the same manner repeatedly over a long period of time. Back problems are by far the most common of the cumulative trauma injuries. Others in this class include the following:

Tenosynovitis—Inflammation of the tendons and their sheaths that occurs in the wrist when there is extreme wrist deviation from side to side.

DeQuervain's Disease—The tendon sheath of both the long and the short abductor muscles of the thumb narrows in this condition.

Trigger Finger—A form of tenosynovitis, trigger finger is a condition imposed when any finger, other than the thumb, must be frequently flexed against resistance.

Video Game Wrist—This condition has had more than seventy-five different symptoms attributed to it, but the underlying cause is the excessive use of control systems associated with video games.

Tendonitis—The muscle-tendon junction and adjacent muscle tissue become inflamed, resulting from repeated abduction of a body member or movement of one body member away from the middle of the body or the member to which it is attached.

Tennis Elbow—Sometimes called epicondylitis, this form of tendinitis is an inflammatory reaction of tissues in the elbow region.

Raynaud's Syndrome—Blood vessels in the hand constrict from cold temperature, vibration, emotion, or unknown causes. Both hands simultaneously become cold, blue, and numb and lose fine manipulative ability. Upon recovery, the hands become red, accompanied by a burning sensation.

TREATMENT

If carpal tunnel syndrome is caught in the initial stages, a splint reinforced with metal is worn for most of the day and night. The splint prevents wrist extension and flexion. Mild anti-inflammatory medications also may be used. In more advanced cases, in addition to the splint, the physician may inject the compartment with a combination of local anesthetic and an anti-inflammatory agent. For patients who for medical reasons cannot be injected, or who have not had a good response to injections, physical therapy may be helpful. The last resort is surgery. Carpal tunnel surgery involves dividing the transverse carpal ligament to relieve pressure on the median nerve. Following surgery, physical therapy to restore strength and flexibility is very important. The best treatment is prevention.

EFFECT ON LIFESTYLE

This syndrome has several adverse consequences. Many patients with carpal tunnel syndrome are unable to differentiate hot from cold by touch and experience an apparent loss of strength in their fingers. They have trouble performing simple tasks such as tying their shoes or picking up small objects.

The most serious effect, however, is on the ability to pursue the chosen field of employment. Medical intervention in carpal tunnel syndrome has met with mixed success. This fact has forced a large number of people to leave a profession they have practiced for many years, to accept an entry level position in another field, or even to join the ranks of the unemployed.

APPEARANCE

There is no outward indication that a person has, or is developing, carpal tunnel syndrome.

ACCOMMODATION

A progressive return to the job is one way to reduce lost time. If employees cannot do the job for which they were trained for eight hours at a time, perhaps they can do it for two hours and something else for the remaining six. As the condition heals, increase the time spent on the primary job. It is important, however, to be sure that the person is not performing the primary job in the same manner that caused the condition.

Modify the layout of the workstation and add fixtures to mount work at angles, thereby reducing the worker's need to bend the wrist or perform the motion that caused the injury. For computer operators, ergonomically correct workstations and keyboards are important.

Consider altering the existing method for performing the job. Rotating workers across jobs that use different muscle groups is one effective way to keep everyone working—and resting at the same time! Provide more frequent rest breaks and encourage stretching and light exercise during breaks. Work practices or workstations need to be changed, but there are no architectural modifications required for this condition.

RESOURCES

There are no support groups or dedicated resource agencies for carpal tunnel syndrome. Information on this condition can be requested from many labor organizations or from insurance carriers. Two booklets, *Preventing Repetitive Motion Injury* and *Preventing Repetitive Strain at the Keyboard*, are available through Krames Communications, 1100 Grundy Lane, San Bruno, CA 94066-3030, (800) 333-3032. Both booklets are excellent means for helping employees understand, and avoid, the dangers of carpal tunnel syndrome.

CEREBRAL PALSY

Classification: Birth Defect, Injury, or Illness

There are 9,000 new cases of cerebral palsy recorded in the United States each year, meaning that an estimated 750,000 Americans have this condition. Though cerebral palsy is usually thought of in relation to children, most children affected with the condition will reach maturity and many will live a normal life span. The number of adults with cerebral palsy is, therefore, increasing rapidly.

Cerebral palsy is a descriptive term that refers to a group of conditions, not a distinct disease. Cerebral refers to the region of the brain that is involved; palsy means shaky or uncontrolled movement. In order to be accurately classified as having cerebral palsy, there must be a problem with movement or posture that occurs early in a child's development, usually before the age of five.

Although genetic causes have not been totally ruled out, most cases of cerebral palsy result from a shortage of oxygen to the developing brain.

This anoxia can be caused by blood incompatibility (Rh factor), umbilical cord problems at birth, excessive smoking or drinking by the mother before birth, or untreated jaundice. Infants and small children can acquire cerebral palsy through accidents, child abuse, or infections such as meningitis.

Many people affected with cerebral palsy have multiple disabling conditions such as seizure disorders; vision, hearing, and speech problems; learning disabilities; and mental health problems. Some types of movement problems may improve with treatment. However, nerve cells are very limited in their power to repair and regenerate so that even when a person appears to have recovered control over the limbs, function is not entirely normal and other deficits will remain. On the other hand, brain damage doesn't get worse.

Cerebral palsy is usually not evident at birth because newborns have little control over their bodies. As development unfolds, normal infants lose the more primitive reflexes and gain fine control over the body's voluntary movements. In contrast, infants with cerebral palsy show a delay in development. The primitive reflexes remain and can dominate behavior to such an extent that the child has difficulty mastering such things as rolling over, sitting, crawling, smiling, or making sounds. Alert parents are often the first to see signs of developmental problems in their child.

Doctors classify cerebral palsy according to the limbs affected and the type of effect. If the legs are primarily affected, it is called diparesis. If only the left or right side is affected, it is called hemiparesis. If both arms and both legs are involved, it is called quadriparesis.

The different types of effect are: spasticity (exaggerated stretch reflexes and a decreased ability to perform precise movements); athetosis (a kind of motion that is slow, involuntary, uncontrolled, unpredictable, and without purpose); ataxia (poor motor coordination stemming from balance and movement inadequacies); and tremors (involuntary vibrating movements that are regular and rhythmic).

TREATMENT

People with cerebral palsy may have a number of problems. Therefore, treatment could include the services of a physical therapist, occupational therapist, speech or language specialist, and physician. Since there is no cure for this condition, the focus will be on developing ability and treating symptoms.

EFFECT ON LIFESTYLE

Cerebral palsy is the third leading cause of the need for assistance with basic life activities and the fifth leading cause of activity limitation. Persons with cerebral palsy may lead independent lives, mildly assisted lifestyles, or may need the help available only in residential development centers. There is no such thing as the "typical" person.

Speech problems affect from 30 to 70 percent of people with cerebral palsy. The impaired communication is often attributed to mental deficiency. However, providing communication boards or computers to replace the spoken word has demonstrated that many persons have intact intelligence though they have unintelligible or barely intelligible speech.

Motor function is a consistent problem for persons with cerebral palsy. It can range from obvious (although minimal) coordination problems to severe involvement in all four limbs and limited trunk control. Fine movements like writing may be impossible for those with hand involvement. Sensory problems such as the loss of ability to identify objects by touch are common. Loss of bowel or bladder control is possible.

The person with cerebral palsy may need to take certain medications regularly.

APPEARANCE

Approximately 66 percent of people with cerebral palsy have the spastic type. They will have tense and contracted muscles that resist movement. If walking is possible, leg movements are stiff, and the gait can resemble the crossed blades of a pair of scissors or cause the person to walk on tiptoe.

Athetoid cerebral palsy results in incessant, slow activity. The hands may turn and twist, and sometimes there is facial grimacing, tonguing, and drooling. There may be abrupt flailing or jerky motions of the body. The unnatural movements and facial expressions of such people are often misinterpreted as signs of mental or emotional disturbance—a mistake to be avoided at any cost. An estimated 20 to 30 percent of people with cerebral palsy have this type.

In cases of ataxic cerebral palsy, the principal movement problem is a lack of balance and coordination. These people may sway when standing, have trouble maintaining their balance, and may walk with their feet spread wide apart to avoid falling.

ACCOMMODATION

The accommodation required must be based on the individual and can range from none at all to a full-time attendant. If there is doubt concerning suitability of the work or school environment, ask the person (or parent) what might need to be adjusted.

RESOURCES

United Cerebral Palsy Association, Inc.
66 East 34th Street
New York, NY 10016

The National Easter Seal Society, Inc.
2023 West Ogden Avenue
Chicago, IL 60612

CORONARY ARTERY DISEASE

Classification: Illness

Coronary artery disease is an umbrella term for various diseases that reduce or halt blood flow in the coronary arteries. This reduced blood flow causes a decrease in oxygen and nutrients available to the heart muscle. The coronary arteries should not be confused with the blood vessels that bring blood to the interior chambers of the heart. The function of the coronary artery system is to maintain an adequate blood supply to the heart muscle (myocardium).

Coronary artery disease is currently the leading cause of death in Europe and the western hemisphere, causing 1.5 million heart attacks and six hundred thousand deaths in the United States alone each year. Typically, coronary artery disease strikes more whites than blacks and more men than women. It is more common in industrial than in underdeveloped countries and affects more affluent than poor people.

Coronary artery disease is a chronic condition of the arteries characterized by abnormal thickening and hardening of the vessel walls resulting in loss of elasticity. There are several identified causes of this disease:

Atherosclerosis—a disease in which fat deposits form in the arteries and obstruct the blood supply
Arteritis—an inflammation of the artery

Coronary artery spasm—a spontaneous, sustained contraction of an artery causing reduced blood supply

Certain infectious diseases

Congenital defects in the heart's vascular system

Whatever the cause, when the heart is starved for the energy it needs to function properly, chest discomfort (angina) is the classic symptom. A crushing tightness, burning, or squeezing sensation is felt in the chest. These painful sensations may radiate to the left arm, neck, jaw, or shoulder blade. The person may also experience nausea, vomiting, or weakness and have cool extremities. Angina is most common after physical exertion but may also occur with emotional excitement, exposure to cold, or overeating.

The difference between angina and acute myocardial infarction (heart attack) is that angina is mild in comparison and does not result in permanent damage to the heart muscle. A heart attack causes an area of the heart muscle to die of starvation. Whether this results in death depends on where the starvation occurs and the amount of tissue involved.

Because coronary aretery disease is so widespread, prevention is of the utmost importance.

TREATMENT

The goal of treatment in angina patients is either to reduce the heart muscle's need for oxygen or to increase oxygen supply. The three most common approaches are nitroglycerin, bypass surgery, and angioplasty.

Nitroglycerin can be given orally, transdermally, or applied to the skin in ointment form.

If the hardened area is extensive, coronary artery bypass surgery is often necessary. In this procedure a piece of vein (usually from the leg) is grafted to the heart and used as a detour around the damaged area.

Angioplasty can be used to compress fat deposits and reduce the blockage in patients with no hardening of the arteries and only partially blocked blood flow. A catheter is inserted in the femoral artery and is then carefully positioned at the blockage. The physician then inserts a small balloon through the catheter to the fat deposit. The balloon is then alternately inflated and deflated until the fat deposit has been flattened enough to permit free flow of bood to the heart. Laser angioplasty, a more recent procedure, is approached the same way, but instead of flattening the fat deposit, the laser melts it away.

EFFECT ON LIFESTYLE

Coronary artery disease usually requires major changes in lifestyle for those who have been diagnosed. Unfortunately, of the approximately six hundred thousand who die annually from heart attacks, sudden death is the first manifestation of disease in 20 to 25 percent of those affected. Therefore, those who are diagnosed are fortunate because making lifestyle changes can make a significant difference in risk.

Among the changes necessary: completely stop cigarette smoking; reduce high blood pressure; reduce cholesterol levels in the blood; increase physical activity; and reduce excess weight. The methods used to achieve these goals will vary from person to person and the success rates of various programs show only that what works for one person will not necessarily work for all.

APPEARANCE

The person with coronary artery disease will not appear any different from peers. A physical examination that includes cardiac testing is required to identify those people at risk.

ACCOMMODATION

A person who experiences angina on exertion should be relieved of all responsibilities that require exertion. If stress or emotional strain is a problem, the person should be allowed to use stress reduction techniques or be transferred to a less stressful atmosphere.

Employers should always be interested in high employee productivity, increased work attendance, reduction in workers compensation claims, and improved health for their workers. The work site, therefore, is an ideal setting for offering preventive health service and health education programs aimed at the prevention of coronary artery disease.

A work site health promotion program involving health education, stress management, physical fitness, weight control, smoking cessation, and the like is a sound investment in productivity for those who are at risk for coronary artery disease.

RESOURCES

American Heart Association
7320 Greenville Avenue
Dallas, TX 75231

American Lung Association
1740 Broadway
New York, NY 10019

CYSTIC FIBROSIS

Classification: Birth Defect

Cystic fibrosis is a hereditary disease that causes secretion of thick mucus in the pancreas and lungs and an excessive salt secretion in the sweat glands. Its basic underlying cause is unknown.

It is estimated that one child in every one thousand Caucasians is born with this disease. It occurs much less frequently in people of African ancestry and is very rarely reported in Oriental children. Although the life span of a child born with the disease has increased steadily, it is the most common fatal genetic disease of white children. Many children with cystic fibrosis succumb before age ten and 80 percent die before age thirty.

Normal mucus is thin, slippery, and clear. In cystic fibrosis the mucus is thick and sticky, which creates two major problems.

First, it clogs the bronchial tubes of the lungs, interfering with breathing; it also lodges in the branches of the windpipe, acting as an obstruction.

In the normal lung, the mucus is constantly being carried away by fine hairs (cilia) that line the walls of the bronchial tubes and the trachea. The mucus is carried along by the rhythmic waving motion of the cilia because it is only a paper-thin, slippery substance. In people with cystic fibrosis, the lungs are poorly cleared because the musus is thick and sticky. As time goes on, more and more mucus remains in the lungs, and some areas become entirely blocked. The air trapped beyond the obstruction will gradually be absorbed into the body, but that area of the lung will collapse and become useless.

The second problem is that mucus plugs up the pancreatic ducts, preventing digestive enzymes from reaching the small intestine. This blockage causes malnutrition. The pancreatic glands will continue to secrete until they are swollen with fluid and become cysts with scarred fibrous tissue surrounding them. A similar but milder process takes place in the liver and results in damage to that organ as well.

The high salt concentration in sweat can bring problems in summer heat or for active people who perspire freely. If enough salt is lost in the sweat, a person can become acutely ill and require hospitalization for the rapid intravenous replacement of the lost salt.

TREATMENT

To offset pancreatic enzyme deficiencies, oral enzymes are taken with meals and snacks. The diet should be low in fat but high in protein and calories. Food requirements for people with cystic fibrosis can be 20 to 50 percent higher than normal. Vitamin supplements are an important part of treatment.

Respiratory care generally consists of the use of inhaled and oral medications and the clearing of mucus by postural drainage and percussion. This procedure involves placing the person on his or her stomach with the head at the lower end of an incline, then firmly slapping the back to help loosen the trapped mucus.

To combat excessive salt loss, people are encouraged to use generous amounts of salt on foods and, during hot weather, additional salt supplements.

EFFECT ON LIFESTYLE

Involvement of the lungs usually results in an increased frequency of respiratory infections that tend to last longer than would be expected and often require hospitalization. Increased food intake and poor digestive ability increase the number of bowel movements each day. In spite of the large food intake, there is little worry about obesity. The person may be on multiple medicines. When lung involvement is at its worst, physical stamina will be impaired. In particularly hot weather it is very important to keep sweaty exercise to a minimum. An adult woman with cystic fibrosis is capable of having children, but adult males are almost always sterile.

APPEARANCE

The person with cystic fibrosis looks and acts essentially normal. Thin extremities are common due to nutrition problems. The chest may have a big or rounded appearance because of the overfilled lungs. Since there is a larger quantity of stool and intestinal gas, the abdomen may be distended and protruding. None of these conditions is so extreme as to be disfiguring.

ACCOMMODATION

There are no structural or mechanical accommodations required for people with cystic fibrosis. Exertion should be kept to a minimum due to reduced lung capacity and to avoid excessive sweating. The person with cystic fibrosis will need to cough frequently to clear the lungs. If the person agrees, peers should be informed that this is not a contagious condition.

RESOURCE

Cystic Fibrosis Foundation
6000 Executive Boulevard, Suite 309
Rockville, MD 20852
(301) 951-4422

DIABETES

Classification: Illness

Diabetes is a disorder of that part of the pancreas called the Islets of Langerhans that secretes insulin, a hormone that allows the body to burn glucose (a form of sugar produced when starches and sugars are digested) for energy. Insulin and another hormone called glucagon, which is also secreted by the pancreas, work together to maintain a relatively steady blood sugar level regardless of what a person eats. Without insulin the unused sugars build up in the blood and eventually overflow into the urine.

An estimated 14 million people in the United States have some form of diabetes. It is more common in women than in men and can begin in childhood or the mature years.

There are two common forms of the disease, called Type I diabetes and Type II diabetes, and some rare forms known as atypical diabetes.

Type I diabetes, also known as insulin-dependent diabetes or juvenile diabetes, begins in the blood. Several years before the disease is diagnosed, antibodies are produced in the blood that attack and destroy the insulin-producing cells in the pancreas. During these years, the person does not exhibit symptoms of diabetes. Eventually, however, the body's insulin production drops below the level required by the body to function effectively. At this point the symptoms of diabetes become apparent.

Type II diabetes, also known as noninsulin-dependent diabetes or adult-onset diabetes, begins in the pancreas. Many years before symptoms appear, the body produces above-normal amounts of insulin. The need to produce ever-increasing amounts of insulin eventually exhausts the insulin-producing ability of the pancreas. Blood sugar levels begin to go out of the normal range, and the symptoms of diabetes begin to manifest themselves.

Atypical diabetes is often found in people who have Type II diabetes that is slowly evolving into Type I. It is also found in people who have scarring in the pancreas as the result of malnutrition or starvation. Because people who have experienced malnutrition or starvation generally do not have ready access to health care, this type of diabetes may be more common than current figures indicate.

TREATMENT

The key to living with diabetes is control. The goal is to achieve the right balance between insulin level, exercise, and food intake, thereby avoiding the problems of blood sugar levels that are too high or too low.

Other than concentrated sweets, people with diabetes can eat the same food the rest of us do. The real difference is that the amount of food eaten and the regularity of meals must be as consistent as possible.

Exercise is a key element in control because it burns sugar without insulin and keeps blood sugar levels down (this can be a two-edged sword). If increased exercise is anticipated the person with diabetes will need to increase food intake. Also important in preventing exercise-induced hypoglycemia is adjusting the location of the insulin injection to the type of exercise. When the exercise is primarily lower limb (such as running), insulin should be injected into the upper limb. When both upper and lower extremities are involved, the injection site should be the abdomen. Using this approach allows the body to absorb the insulin at a steady rate instead of accelerating the process by "pumping" the muscle that has received the injection.

The number of insulin injections and the dosage of each must be carefully controlled. Insulin is given by injection because if it is taken by mouth, the body's digestive juices destroy it. Insulin injected under the skin can be slowly absorbed into the bloodstream. An insulin-dependent diabetic never injects insulin directly into a vein.

Regular blood glucose monitoring is part of the diabetic's daily life. Usually a drop of blood from an earlobe or finger stick is placed on a chemically treated strip, which is then put into a meter for a blood sugar reading. Another method relies on a visual comparison of the color change taking place on the strip with a color-coded chart.

Urine tests are used to monitor ketones, whose presence in the urine is a warning sign of ketoacidosis that can lead to diabetic coma. This is a simple test that involves dipping a chemically treated strip of paper into a urine sample and then comparing the strip to a color-coded chart.

EFFECT ON LIFESTYLE

Most people have heard of diabetic coma or insulin reaction—two problems associated with diabetes. However, diabetes is also associated with other severe and often life-threatening complications, including myocardial infarctions, cerebrovascular accidents, kidney disease, blindness, premature atherosclerosis, neurological disorders, and lower limb amputations. Uncontrolled diabetes contributes to both premature birth and stillbirth.

Insulin reaction, or insulin shock, can be caused by injecting too much insulin (which results in extremely low blood sugar), delaying or skipping meals, overexercising, or experiencing extreme stress. The first symptoms of hypoglycemia include anxiety, sweating, rapid heart rate, trembling, shakiness, hunger, dizziness, cold and clammy skin, nausea, headache, and fatigue. The downward spiral can be stopped at this point if the person drinks fruit juice or a carbonated soft drink (not diet) or eats candy or honey.

If the blood sugar content continues to get lower the person will experience sluggish thinking, muscle weakness, drowsiness, blurred or double vision, unconsciousness, and/or convulsions. This person needs medical help quickly.

Diabetic coma (also called ketoacidosis) results when there is insufficient insulin for the amount of sugar in the blood. The sugar in the blood cannot be used for energy and so it is excreted in the urine. When the body can't get energy from sugar, it then turns to fat and protein for food. The breakdown of fat releases acids in the blood, and ketoacidosis soon follows.

Some of the causes of ketoacidosis are forgetting to take insulin or taking too little; onset of infection or mild illness; overeating or excessive intake of alcoholic beverages; and emotional stress. A simple cold or fever complicates a diabetic's metabolism, increasing the required insulin by as much as one-third.

Warning symptoms of an impending diabetic coma begin gradually and include extreme thirst, loss of appetite, nausea, vomiting, abdominal pain, leg cramps, nervousness, dimness of vision, flushed skin, and a fruity odor to the breath. This person needs medical help immediately. An impending diabetic coma is an emergency.

When the body is using fat (lipids) for energy instead of sugar, there is the potential for damage to the blood vessels. As lipids are transported by the blood from storage depots to the hungry cells, lipid particles are deposited on the walls of the blood vessels. These deposits lead to atherosclerosis ("fat" deposits on the walls of the blood vessels that obstruct the flow of blood) and a multitude of other problems related to the circulatory system.

In addition, diabetics have small vessel (microvascular) changes that are not seen in nondiabetics. These small vessel changes commonly cause problems with the kidneys, eyes, nervous system, and skin.

People with nerve damage due to diabetes may not be able to feel a blister on their feet. A simple blister, combined with reduced blood flow, can lead to serious problems if not attended to. Amputation of toes, feet, or even the leg itself is not uncommon.

Children who develop diabetes before age four are at greater risk for neurocognitive impairment and may have significantly lower intelligence than their peers. A child who develops diabetes after age five and is considered to be an underachiever may have experienced numerous school absences that contributed to poor performance; but the poor performance is not the direct result of diabetes.

APPEARANCE

The person with diabetes appears entirely normal while the disease is well controlled. However, if blood sugar escapes normal levels the result will be either insulin shock or diabetic coma. Some people whose diabetes has not been well controlled in the past may have amputated lower extremities. Diabetes can also lead to blindness.

ACCOMMODATIONS

There are no physical accommodations required for the person who has diabetes only. However, some people who have diabetes have had an amputation or are blind as a result of the disease. Accommodations will need to be made for these conditions.

RESOURCE

American Diabetes Association
2 Park Avenue
New York, NY 10016

DOWN SYNDROME

Classification: Birth Defect

One out of every 650 babies—15,000 per year—is born with Down syndrome. Down syndrome is a congenital condition that yields varying degrees of mental retardation and multiple defects, including congenital heart conditions.

Until 1959 almost nothing was known about this syndrome; then it was discovered that people with Down syndrome have forty-seven chromosomes in each cell instead of the normal forty-six. The extra chromosome is on the twenty-first pair; thus, the term "trisomy 21" is sometimes used to describe this syndrome. The cause of the abnormality is unknown (see Figure 2).

Figure 2
The Etiology of Down Syndrome

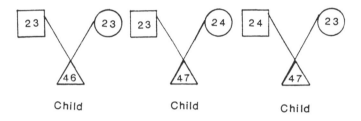

Normally, egg and sperm cells each have 23 chromosomes to contribute to the fetus. In the case of a child with Down syndrome, either the egg or the sperm cell contributes 24 chromosomes. The extra chromosome causes the mental and physical characteristics of Down syndrome.

Those people who are at high risk for having a child born with this condition are those who carry the chromosomal defect themselves or who have been exposed to gene-damaging substances such as viruses, X-rays, or chemicals. Women and men of very young or advanced age are most likely to have a child with Down syndrome. Studies have shown that a girl younger than fifteen has the same statistical risk as a woman of thirty-five (a one in four hundred chance) of having a baby with Down syndrome. When a woman reaches forty-eight, the chance is one in twelve that she will have an affected child. The genetic problem that causes Down syndrome can originate in the father as well as the mother, but the significance of the father's age is still unclear.

Newborn infants born with Down syndrome are, anatomically speaking, unfinished. All of the systems in the body show major deficiencies in development. Physical growth is abnormally slow and will cease entirely at an early age.

Intellectual ability is severely limited and tends to drop during early adolescence. During puberty, definite changes in intellectual ability may occur; the person may have a more difficult time learning and may become less attentive. The cause of this deterioration is unknown, but research seems to connect it with Alzheimer's disease. Researchers have observed that people born with Down syndrome tend to age prematurely.

Life expectancy for people with Down syndrome has increased greatly due to improved treatment for the related complications. Nearly one in four persons lives to age fifty or older. Nevertheless, nearly one-third die before they are ten years old. The cause of very early death is usually congenital heart disease.

TREATMENT

Medical and surgical treatment of the life-threatening congenital defects frequently associated with Down syndrome are essential to the child's optimal health. At this time, there are no known medical regimens that can reverse the pattern of developmental delays and disabilities evident in Down syndrome.

EFFECT ON LIFESTYLE

Most people with Down syndrome are developmentally delayed and intellectually compromised. They *do* understand that they are different from other people and are often hurt when referred to as retarded or by other such labels.

The abnormally small mouth and protruding tongue, which are characteristic, produce a tendency to "mouth breathe." People who mouth breathe are more susceptible to upper respiratory infections. People with Down syndrome usually have small teeth in abnormal and maloccluded alignment that can lead to many dental and oral hygiene problems.

They also have very poor tactile and fine motor discrimination. Balance is a problem for those with Down syndrome. Many of those affected cannot balance on one foot for more than a few seconds and cannot balance at all with their eyes closed.

Demonstrating a good memory, many can acquire a large vocabulary, read at the primary level, and learn to spell relatively well. Students often give the impression of knowing more than they do because of their great gift for mimicry, which gives them the ability to say or do something with no knowledge of its meaning.

People with Down syndrome are often as eager to leave home as normal young adults. They may choose to live in a variety of settings and are often capable of working in the competitive labor market in jobs that don't impose unrealistic demands on the intellect.

The social maturity of persons with Down syndrome is always more than their mental age. They are often described as well mannered, responsible, cooperative, honest, cheerful, and friendly. They like routine and many resist changes with uncharacteristic stubbornness.

APPEARANCE

There are more than fifty signs and symptoms associated with Down syndrome, many of which are readily apparent. Most common are slanting, almond-shaped eyes; protruding tongue; small, open mouth; flat nasal bridge; abnormal or missing teeth; flattened face; small external ears; short neck; short stature; short extremities with broad, flat, squarish hands and feet; low muscle tone; dry, inelastic skin; and mental retardation.

ACCOMMODATION

The accommodation necessary for a person with Down syndrome usually centers on intellectual ability rather than physical ability. Even individuals with severe disability can be employed in a variety of jobs as long as they are not required to think and act quickly. Jobs requiring fine motor skills, strength, or physical exertion are not suitable. Companies that employ people with Down syndrome usually find that they have employed honest, willing, dependable people.

RESOURCES

Down Syndrome Congress
1640 West Roosevelt Road, Room 156-E
Chicago, IL 60608

March of Dimes Birth Defects Foundation
1275 Mamaroneck Avenue
White Plains, NY 10605

EMPHYSEMA

Classification: Illness

Emphysema symptoms usually appear during the fifth decade of life. Though emphysema is not curable, there are treatments available to help people live with it more comfortably and for a longer period of time. It is a destructive disease for hundreds of thousands of people and is third among the diseases for which Social Security gives disability benefits. In 1986 (the most recent year for which statistics are available) 72,000 people in the United States died from this condition—and the number of deaths has been steadily increasing for the past ten years. The death rate is twice as high for males as for females, and three times higher in white people than in black people. In countries where smoking—the major cause of emphysema—is even more common than in the United States, the number of people with emphysema is significantly higher.

Emphysema is an abnormal condition that causes destructive changes in the alveolar walls that lead to overinflation of the lungs, resulting in a loss of lung elasticity and decreased ability to exchange gases. Chronic emphysema is usually accompanied by chronic bronchitis. The two conditions together are referred to as chronic obstructive pulmonary disease.

Current research indicates that cigarette smoke triggers a chemical chain reaction in the lungs, the end result of which is a release of enzymes that attack the elastic cells of the alveolar wall. The alveoli are the small sacs at the end of the airway where gases are exchanged between the lungs and the bloodstream. As elasticity is lost, air is trapped in these sacks and continues to accumulate, sometimes causing the tiny sacks to tear. When the alveoli are distended with air, they push against the blood vessels, thereby constricting the flow of blood and further reducing the effective exchange of gases. Additionally, the heart must work harder to pump blood through the constricted vessels. The heart may enlarge under the strain and eventually give out.

While cigarette smoking is the main cause of emphysema, second-hand smoke, polluted metropolitan air, allergens, and occupational hazards all contribute to the development and exacerbation of emphysema.

TREATMENT

Oxygen therapy is the only treatment that significantly reduces the symptoms and improves the survival rate of people with severe end-stage emphysema. Oxygen therapy not only allows patients to exercise for longer periods, but it can have a positive effect on their psychological condition. Portable tanks supply oxygen by gas or liquid system. These can be used in the office as well as in the home.

Portable concentrators that filter nitrogen from the air and provide nearly pure oxygen are also available. The most common way to administer oxygen is by nasal cannula, but a transtracheal catheter improves oxygen delivery and is sometimes used.

Because of the poor prognosis and progressive decline associated with emphysema, early diagnosis and rapid treatment are essential.

EFFECT ON LIFESTYLE

The most important thing the person must do is to give up smoking. This is not an easy adjustment for most people. The person will be encouraged to drink a large amount of fluid daily. Activity is encouraged to the limit of the person's tolerance. Fatigue, constipation, and upper respiratory tract infection and irritation are to be avoided. A respirator and oxygen equipment may be prescribed for the person to use. People with emphysema are more apt to contract severe infections of the respiratory tract, such as pneumonia or influenza.

APPEARANCE

Affected people may have shortness of breath, difficulty breathing except when sitting or standing upright, generalized difficulty breathing, cough, a bluish-purple discoloration of the skin, unequal chest expansion, abnormal rapid breathing rate, and an elevated temperature. Anxiety, restlessness, confusion, weakness, anorexia, congestive heart failure, pulmonary edema, and respiratory failure are common in advanced cases, as are fatigue and malaise. People with emphysema often purse their lips during exhalation in a response that prevents premature collapse of the airways. The exertion from this labored breathing contributes to weight loss and malnutrition.

ACCOMMODATION

People with an increased fluid intake may need more restroom breaks than normal. It would be wise to have the work area as close as possible to this rest area to prevent unnecessary exertion. Stair climbing, heavy lifting, or exertion are to be avoided.

RESOURCE

American Lung Association
1740 Broadway
New York, NY 10019

EPILEPSY

Classification: Birth Defect or Injury

The preferred term for epilepsy is seizure disorder. A seizure is a physical disorder caused by sudden changes in how the brain functions. When brain cells activate at rapid, random rates, a person's consciousness and actions are changed for a brief time. These physical changes are called seizures.

About two million people have seizure disorders. Most of these have no known cause. Among the known causes are head injuries, brain tumors, genetic conditions, lead poisoning, problems occurring before birth, and illnesses like encephalitis or meningitis. Seizure disorders are never contagious.

Seizures originate in the brain when normal electrical signals between the cells are disrupted. The cells begin to fire in a rapid, disorganized manner, which may afffect only a local area or travel throughout the entire brain. This condition lasts from a few seconds to a minute or two, then ends by itself when naturally occurring inhibitor chemicals in the brain bring activity back to normal.

There are four common forms of seizure.

A *tonic-clonic seizure* (also called grand mal seizure or convulsive seizure) begins when air is suddenly forced out of the lungs, resulting in a hoarse cry. The person will then lose consciousness and fall down. The body will stiffen briefly (the tonic phase) and then begin making jerking movements (the clonic phase). Bladder or bowel control is sometimes lost during the clonic portion of the seizure. A frothy saliva may develop around the mouth, and the tongue is occasionally bitten. Breathing may be barely noticeable or even stop for a few moments, causing a bluish color in the skin. The jerking motions will then begin to slow down, and the seizure will end by itself after a minute or two. When the person regains consciousness, a feeling of confusion or sleepiness may be present. Most people can go back to their normal activities after a brief recovery period.

An *absence seizure* (often called a petit mal seizure) looks like daydreaming or simply a blank stare. These are most often seen in children and last only a few seconds. A person having this type of seizure is not aware of people or things in the vicinity and may stumble or fall if walking during the seizure. Occasionally these seizures cause blinking or chewing movements, head turning, or arm waving.

A *psycho-motor seizure* (temporal lobe seizure or complex partial seizure) occurs when the extra brain activity remains in just one area of the brain. This kind of seizure starts out with a strange sensation—fear, feeling sick in the stomach, or seeing and hearing something that isn't there. Then the person will develop a blank stare. A movement pattern will then begin. There is usually a set pattern of involuntary movements that the person goes through every time a seizure occurs, though the pattern varies from person to person.

People having this type of seizure may follow directions if they are given in a quiet, calm voice, although they are not truly aware of things and people around them. The seizure will last for a minute or two, but full awareness may not return for quite some time. It is not unusual for the person to be confused and irritable during recovery and there will be no memory of the event or what happened while the seizure was occurring.

There is no single things that triggers a seizure, though many people are susceptible to flickering lights. Anger, fright, bad news, and other high stress factors have been known to precipitate seizures. Many women have seizures only around the time of their period. This is caused by the edema many women experience during the menses. Seizures happen more often if a person is very tired or has missed taking seizure medication.

Many people experience an aura before a major seizure begins (medically speaking, the aura is in fact part of the seizure). The aura often gives the person time to move away from possible hazards and to inform people nearby that a seizure is beginning. Sometimes the seizure does not spread and all the person experiences is the aura.

The actions of people having a seizure are involuntary. However, if they are grabbed or held down they may instinctively lash out and injure those restraining them. Intentional violence does not occur.

TREATMENT

Seizure disorders can be treated with drugs, surgery, or special diets. Drug treatment is by far the most common. With proper care, 80 to 85 percent of people with seizure disorders can maintain control of seizures so long as medication is taken routinely. Surgery is used if the seizures are caused by tumors or if they begin in a small area of the brain that can be identified and removed. A diet high in fats (a ketogenic diet) is usually tried after drugs have failed to control the seizures. The diet produces a chemical condition in the body which, in some instances, will prevent seizures.

EFFECT ON LIFESTYLE

The average seizure does not have any lasting effect. Occasionally, a person having a seizure may fall in such a way that breathing is blocked or have a heart attack as a result of the stress involved. A seizure is very seldom the cause of death. Most deaths due to seizures result from a series of nonstop seizures that last for hours if not treated at a hospital. Anyone who has more than one convulsive seizure in a short span of time should receive immediate medical attention.

People with seizure disorders generally show a normal range of intelligence: some are very intelligent, most are average, some are slow learners.

People with seizure disorders can take part in sports or other vigorous activity if seizure control is generally good. The type of sport should be carefully considered, however, because water and airborne sports present more of a danger during a seizure than land-based sports. Research has suggested that people have fewer seizures when they are actively occupied.

The excessive use of alcohol is likely to make seizures worse and even moderate use depends on the individual. Many doctors advise people with seizure disorder to avoid alcohol altogether.

ACCOMMODATION

First aid for seizure disorder is very simple: keep the person safe until the seizure stops by itself. Some things to remember for convulsive seizures:

1. Keep yourself and those around you calm.
2. Remove hard or sharp items from the area near the person.
3. Loosen ties or choker-type necklaces that may impede breathing.
4. Turn the person onto his or her side. (This helps keep the airway clear.)
5. Do not force the mouth open. It is not true that people having a seizure will swallow their tongue.
6. Don't attempt to stop the movements.

7. Don't attempt artificial respiration during the seizure. (Artificial respiration should only be used if the person doesn't start breathing after the seizure is over.)
8. Don't leave the person unattended.
9. After the seizure ends, act in a calm, reassuring manner.
10. If the person remains confused, offer whatever help is appropriate.

If you know the person has epilepsy, it is not usually necessary to call an ambulance unless the event lasts longer than a few minutes, another seizure begins soon after the first, or the person cannot be awakened after the movements have stopped.

Some things to remember for absence seizures that involve automatic movements:

1. Explain to others what is happening so they do not think the person is drunk or on drugs.
2. Speak to the person in a quiet, calm manner.
3. Guide the person away from danger.
4. Don't grab or restrain the person. Instinct may cause struggling or lashing out.
5. Stay with the person until awareness returns, and offer any appropriate help.

The person with a seizure disorder is fully mobile and needs no physical accommodations. It may be advisable to keep hot surfaces and hard, sharp edges to a minimum to reduce the possibility of injury during a fall.

RESOURCE

Epilepsy Foundation of America
1828 L Street, NW, Suite 406
Washington, DC 20036

FETAL ALCOHOL SYNDROME

Classification: Birth Defect

Approximately 40,000 babies are born each year with problems resulting from maternal alcohol use during pregnancy. About 7,000 of these infants have fetal alcohol syndrome, a condition so severe that the child will have lifelong behavioral, intellectual, and physical problems. The other 33,000 children will suffer from less severe effects such as "attention deficit disorders," speech and language problems, and hyperactivity. Fetal alcohol syndrome is the leading known cause of mental retardation in the United States. It is entirely preventable.

When a pregnant woman drinks, the alcohol passes directly through the placenta to the baby. The baby's immature organs are unable to break down the alcohol quickly so the blood alcohol level in the baby is higher than in the mother.

TREATMENT

Treatment has to focus on the developmental potential of each child. The educational, occupational, and social abilities of the child must be appraised and professionals in each area will be required to address the unique problems of fetal alcohol syndrome. At present there are no medical interventions available to reverse or mitigate the problems of fetal alcohol syndrome.

EFFECT ON LIFESTYLE

Children may have better expressive language than receptive language; they may be able to start a conversation, but be unable to respond appropriately to a question. This problem can extend into adulthood, depending on the extent of the neurological damage.

Even those who are not technically retarded have a lifelong problem with socialization and communication skills. They demonstrate a lack of initiative, often fail to consider the consequences of their actions, are unresponsive to social cues, and have difficulty in making friends.

Many people who are retarded have increasing behavior problems as they mature; however, adolescents and adults with fetal alcohol syndrome have more severe levels of maladaptive behavior. Few are capable of becoming independent adults in terms of both housing and income.

APPEARANCE

Babies born with fetal alcohol syndrome are abnormally small at birth. Often they have small, widely spaced eyes; short, upturned nose; and small, flat cheeks. They have a small head compared to body size and are likely to have mental retardation, learning disabilities, and perceptual disorders. As the child grows into adulthood, some of these problems are mitigated and some are exacerbated. Facial anomalies often disappear as the child grows to adulthood. However, adults tend to be shorter than their peers and have heads that are small in relation to body size. Hyperactivity is a constant problem.

ACCOMMODATION

Since there is no physical disability involved with fetal alcohol syndrome, architectural accommodation is not required. If the adult is to be employed, it will need to be in a routine, nondistracting, supportive atmosphere.

RESOURCES

March of Dimes
1275 Mamaroneck Avenue
White Plains, NY 10605

Fetal Alcohol Education Program
Boston University School of Medicine
7 Kent Street
Brookline, MA 02146

FRIEDREICH'S ATAXIA

Classification: Birth Defect

There are about 8,600 people in the United States with Friedreich's ataxia and about 150,000 people with various other types of hereditary ataxia.

The word "ataxia" means "without order" and comes from the Greek word *ataxia*. The hereditary ataxias include a broad range of changes occurring within the nervous system, but they can be divided into two main types—those that are dominantly inherited and those that are recessively inherited.

Friedreich's ataxia is a recessively inherited abnormality. This means that the abnormal gene must be present in both parents in order for the condition to manifest itself in their child. The exact chemical abnormality in the gene responsible for Friedreich's ataxia has not yet been discovered. There is no test to identify carriers or to detect the presence of Friedreich's in a child before birth. The condition affects boys and girls equally often.

Symptoms usually begin in childhood or youth, between the ages of seven and thirteen, as the result of deterioration in the area of the brain that controls muscle coordination, the spinal cord, and the nerves.

Balance and coordination are affected first. What may just appear to be clumsy movements may not be correctly diagnosed until symptoms become more pronounced, often over a period of several years. Coordination of both arms and legs is affected. Walking will become difficult and is characterized by feet placed far apart to compensate for poor balance. The spine may begin to curve to one side, and the feet may become rigid or deformed. There may be numbness and loss of sensation in all parts of the body. Eventually a wheelchair will become necessary. Some people experience vision and hearing problems. Lack of coordination in the hands and arms affects the person's ability to perform tasks that require fine motor control such as writing and eating.

Ataxia can often affect speech and swallowing. The fear of choking becomes very real when the ability to swallow and cough has been affected. The person with Friedreich's ataxia needs to take special precautions to prevent the inhaling of fluids and secretions.

A few people with Friedreich's ataxia have mental impairment. This is often in the area of information processing, which is slowed by the disease, not in the area of understanding. Diabetes is present in many people, and in some, the heart muscles may be weakened. Most ataxias are progressive, but they are not always fatal and do not always result in total disability. Ataxia can shorten the life span due to possible heart or respiratory complications.

Occasionally Friedreich's ataxia appears to have become arrested; these remissions may last five to ten years or longer. However, in the majority of cases the disease is slowly but steadily progressive. Most people are seriously incapacitated within twenty years of the appearance of the first symptoms; however, some people manifest only one or two symptoms and are minimally affected during their entire life span. With good medical treatment the average life span is steadily increasing from its former thirty-six years. Nearly 75 percent of the deaths attributed to the disease are from heart failure.

TREATMENT

There is no specific treatment or cure for Friedreich's ataxia at the present. However, treatment is available for the heart problems and diabetes associated with the condition. Surgery can alleviate scoliosis, and orthopedic appliances along with physical therapy can prolong the ability to walk.

EFFECT ON LIFESTYLE

When the disease manifests itself in the first decade of life, the child is often ostracized by peers or becomes the recipient of taunting. Frequent falling or a drunken-like gait can contribute to social isolation for those affected in the second decade of life when this behavior is mistaken for an alcoholic or a drug-induced condition.

Loss of fine motor control will produce handwriting that is difficult to read. Tremor of the upper limbs may become so great that self-feeding becomes impossible. A loss of the sense of "place in space" will result in over- or undershooting when reaching for something or moving toward or away from something. Lack of coordination in the eyes will result in difficulty with visual tracking and can cause reluctance or inability to read. There is no loss of bowel or bladder control, though hygiene may be affected by the lack of coordination.

APPEARANCE

The person with Friedreich's ataxia will appear to be clumsy or even drunk. When walking over an obstacle, they tend to lift their feet too high. Deformities such as clubfoot, hammer toe, kyphosis, or scoliosis are often present. Involuntary side-to-side movement of the eyes is almost always present.

ACCOMMODATION

If the person is ambulatory, minimize sharp corners and large glass areas in case of falls. Stair climbing should be minimal. If ramps are used, be sure there are handrails to aid with balance. If a wheelchair is necessary, check for accessibility in all areas.

Tasks requiring fine motor skills should be avoided or mechanical devices to accomplish the work will need to be provided.

One or two "buddies" should be identified who can assure the person's safety in case an emergency requires evacuation of the work area.

RESOURCES

Friedreich's Ataxia Group in America
P.O. Box 11116
Oakland, CA 94611

National Ataxia Foundation
6681 Country Club Drive
Minneapolis, MN 55427

Muscular Dystrophy Association
810 Seventh Avenue
New York, NY 10019

GUILLAIN-BARRÉ

Classification: Illness

Guillain-Barré is an inflammatory disease of the nerves and muscles that causes rapid loss of strength and sensation. The onset of symptoms is rapid and often occurs a few weeks after a mild viral infection. Because this condition strikes only two people in one hundred thousand each year, very little is known about it.

Guillain-Barré results from inflammation and destruction of the myelin sheath that surrounds nerves. Once sections of this insulating material are gone, the nerves are short-circuited and the signals from the brain can't get through. The nerve damage is thought to be the result of an abnormal immune reaction that causes the body to attack the myelin much the same as happens in multiple sclerosis. There are two main differences between Guillian-Barré and multiple sclerosis. First, multiple sclerosis attacks the central nervous system whereas Guillain-Barré attacks the peripheral nerves. Second, in Guillain-Barré the body does not form hardened patches (sclerosis) over the damaged area; therefore, the body is able to regenerate the damaged myelin.

The first symptoms of Guillain-Barré are often described as tingling, pins and needles, or vibrating in the fingers, hands, toes, or feet—rapidly progressing to weakness of those areas and then to paralysis. The face muscles may be paralyzed as well. In severe cases, paralysis of respiratory muscles occurs, requiring a tracheostomy and artificial ventilation. The speed with which the muscles are paralyzed is an important factor in this condition. Some people end up in an intensive care unit within twenty-four hours.

The exact cause of Guillain-Barré is unknown. At present there is no cure for the condition, but most people recover completely in anywhere from two months to two years.

TREATMENT

There is no specific treatment for Guillian-Barré. Plasmapheresis (a procedure that removes blood plasma and replaces it with donated plasma) is used if the nerves to the heart or lungs begin to fail. Doctors will sometimes choose to do complete blood transfusions in very small children. Plasma or blood exchange, in addition to being time-consuming and expensive, is not without risk and thus is used only in extreme cases. Recovery is generally assisted through the use of supportive measures such as artificial ventilation, intravenous feeding, and physical therapy.

EFFECT ON LIFESTYLE

This illness can strike with terrifying swiftness. Depending on the severity of the attack, the person can spend anywhere from a few days to many months in a hospital. During the acute phase of the illness, the person may be unable to breathe without mechanical help, talk, eat, or sit up. As the recovery process begins, the person will progress from being very weak and totally dependent, to using a wheelchair, then perhaps a walker, then fully recovered. Recovery can be very slow.

APPEARANCE

People recovering from Guillain-Barré will look like they have had a spinal cord injury. However, because they know the prognosis for a full recovery is good, they may not have the adjustment problems often seen in people with spinal cord injury. They will have some weakness in the affected limbs and may use a wheelchair or walker.

ACCOMMODATION

When people are ready to return to their former lifestyle, they will need to be as active as muscle strength permits. Since most people make a full recovery from Guillain-Barré it usually isn't necessary to make long-term adjustments in the workplace.

RESOURCES

There are no specific support groups in existence at this time. A physician who specializes in neurology should be consulted for further information.

HEARING DISORDERS

Classification: Birth Defect, Illness, or Injury

Nearly 2 million Americans are either totally deaf or suffer such significant hearing loss that they cannot hear normal conversation, traffic noises, a ringing phone, or a fire alarm. Each year over two hundred thousand children are either born deaf or lose their hearing during the first year of life.

All of these people experience the frustration of trying to communicate in a hearing world. Human communication is essential to learning, working, and social interaction. Hearing loss can affect every aspect of a person's life. Yet it is often referred to as the "hidden disability" because it has no visible manifestations.

Human hearing depends on a series of events that converts sound waves in the air into electrical impulses carried along nerves to the brain. Sound is a form of energy. If you stamp your foot, the impact generates a force that presses against the molecules of air. The molecules are pushed outward, much like the circles formed when a pebble is dropped into a pond. The air molecules don't continue outward like the circles, however. Air "circles" vibrate back and forth.

The number of vibrations per second determines the frequency of the sound. Human beings interpret the frequency of sound as pitch: the greater the frequency, the higher the pitch. The intensity of sound, or loudness, is measured by how far the molecules move back and forth as they vibrate.

The function of the outer ear is to pick up sound waves and conduct them accurately to the inner ear. When sound waves are collected by the outer ear, they travel for about an inch down a narrow tube, in order to strike the eardrum, or tympanic membrane. The eardrum is shaped like a broad flat cone, and it vibrates in rhythm with the sound waves striking it. The function of the eardrum is to transmit the vibrations accurately to the three tiny bones (the ossicles) in the middle ear. The ossicles are the smallest bones in the human body. Their job is to amplify the vibrations so that they can pass on to the inner ear.

As the three tiny bones vibrate, the bone farthest in presses against a membrane called the oval window. This window is encased in a thin shell of bone that spirals to form the snail-shaped cochlea. The smallest compartment of the cochlea contains the organ of hearing. This organ (the organ of Corti) contains special cells that transform the vibrations into electrical impulses that are carried along the auditory nerve to the brain.

In the brain, the signals are conducted to the cortex, the outermost covering of the brain, which contains the centers associated with interpreting speech and music.

The process of hearing is so complex that it has been divided into two categories for the purpose of identifying problems. Conductive problems are those that originate in the outer and middle ear. Sensorineural problems are those that extend from the inner ear to the brain.

Among the most common conductive problems are the following:

Perforated eardrum—a hole or tear caused by an injury or infection. Doctors can repair or even rebuild a perforated eardrum.

Malformations—hereditary conditions, injuries, or illnesses that occur before or at birth. These can sometimes be repaired.

Otitis media—a middle ear disease common in children but occurring at any age. If the condition is chronic, the physician may insert a small drainage tube in the eardrum to relieve pressure until medication clears the underlying infection.

Otosclerosis—an overgrowth of bone in the middle ear. Surgery can remove the excess bone and if necessary an artificial bone can be implanted to replace the entire part.

Presbycusis—hearing loss associated with the outer and middle ear and age.

Among the most frequent sensorineural problems are the following:

Hereditary disorders—a wide range of conditions that result in deafness at birth or later in life. These are usually not treatable.

Hearing loss at birth—caused by difficult delivery or an illness or infection passed from the mother to the unborn baby.

Trauma—any insult to the head that affects the ear, auditory nerve, or brain.

Noise damage—prolonged exposure to loud noise can cause permanent damage that ends in deafness.

TREATMENT

When surgical repair of the ear can restore all or part of the ability to hear, it is the procedure of choice. When surgery isn't an option, a hearing aid to amplify sound may be the solution. Hearing aids can benefit anyone who has some residual hearing. A hearing aid's effectiveness depends on how well it is designed and on how well the aid matches the person's needs. A hearing aid is not an instant cure. It takes time and a period of adjustment to get the most out of the device. If a person is profoundly deaf, nothing will bring sound into his or her world.

EFFECT ON LIFESTYLE

The effect that hearing loss has on a person's life depends on how young he or she was when hearing was lost and on how complete the loss is.

The child who has never heard speech cannot be expected to talk without extensive training. Even if the child is taught to speak, understanding what is said is a major challenge. Only about one-third of spoken English can be understood by lip-reading alone.

As the child becomes an adult, communication and social barriers continue to work against achieving his or her full potential. Most people with hearing impairment have the intelligence and creativity to succeed at any profession they choose, but being deaf is a very isolating disability. It's like being a tourist in a land whose language you don't understand: there is nothing wrong with the native or tourist, but communicating is a struggle that often makes the tourist glad to get "back to his own." Even with the communication aids available today, 95 percent of deaf people prefer the company of other deaf people.

If hearing loss occurs after the ability to talk was strong, the person can then retain the ability by using it. This person may talk very loudly without intention or may whisper because of the fear of being loud.

Sign language has been an area of disagreement among people who are deaf. Some people feel everyone should learn to talk, some feel they should be taught to sign exact English, and others advocate American Sign Language (Ameslan). Ameslan uses combinations of hand, face, and body movements to comprise a vocabulary and grammar that are distinct from English. Because of this disagreement, not all people who are deaf can communicate with each other.

ACCOMMODATION

An increasing number of technological devices are available for the hearing-impaired. Telephones and teleprinters are fairly common and, since the Americans with Disabilities Act, required in some places.

The day-to-day communication problems between hearing and non-hearing people can be reduced with a few simple accommodations.

Light is important to someone who relies on visual cues. Eliminate any flickering and glaring illumination. Light should be on the face of the speaker, not in the eyes of the deaf person. Don't sit in front of a light source because it creates a silhouette effect that masks facial expressions and lip movements. Leave some light in the room when showing slides or video tapes.

Background noise interferes with the ability to understand speech that is amplified by a hearing aid. Eliminate background music, and reduce things like movement of chairs and building noise.

Face a hearing-impaired person directly when speaking, since it is impossible to lip-read from the side. Refrain from eating, chewing gum, placing objects in or near the mouth, and covering the mouth in any way as this interferes with communication. Beards and mustaches also hide important facial clues and mouth movements. Speak clearly at a moderate speed, and never overemphasize mouth motions.

If an interpreter is being used to facilitate communication, he or she should sit directly beside the speaker, facing the person who is hearing-impaired. When addressing the nonhearing person through an interpreter, forget the presence of the interpreter. Do not say "Ask him if he wants . . ."; say, "Do you want . . ." It is inappropriate to ask an interpreter anything about the client. Interpreters function under a strict code of ethics regarding confidentiality of client information. The code also requires that interpreters repeat everything that is being said, including side comments or telephone conversations received by hearing persons during their presence. So be aware that anything that is said within the room will be repeated to the client.

Of course, the ultimate accommodation is to learn sign language and communicate directly with the person. Ameslan is a graceful, easy language to learn.

RESOURCES

Alexander Graham Bell Association for the Deaf, Inc.
3417 Volta Place, NW
Washington, DC 20007
(202) 337-5220

National Association for the Deaf
814 Thayer Avenue, Suite 301
Silver Spring, MD 20910
(301) 587-1788

HEMOPHILIA

Classification: Birth Defect

There are at least eight different bleeding disorders grouped under the term "hemophilia." The term is used to describe a condition in which blood clots form very slowly or not at all. Historically, it was said that hemophilia occurred only in males and was transmitted through females. Recently, however, a type of hemophilia has been identified in women.

There are two types of hemophilia that account for approximately 90 percent of the serious bleeding disorders encountered: Hemophilia A is caused by a deficiency in clotting Factor VIII and Hemophilia C is a deficiency in clotting Factor XI.

There are eleven clotting substances, identified by the Roman numerals I through XI. These clotting proteins are molecules that circulate in the blood, and their presence is essential to form a clot and stop the flow of blood. A deficiency of any one of these substances can cause a serious bleeding problem.

When skin is broken and blood is exposed to tissue other than the lining of a blood vessel, a series of events is activated to prevent excessive blood loss. The first reaction is a change in the blood vessel itself. Whenever a blood vessel is injured, small bundles of muscle fibers that surround the vessel contract and decrease its size. Depending on the strength of the contraction, blood flow will either slow down or cease completely. After a short period the muscles will relax; if an adequate clot has not formed, bleeding will begin again.

The second event is formation of a "platelet plug." Platelets are cells that float in the blood. They are designed to adhere to any tissue other than the lining of a normal blood vessel. When a vessel is broken, platelets adhere to the underlying tissue and plug the opening to prevent blood loss. They accomplish this in two ways: they attract more platelets to the area; and they release enzymes that aid in the formation of a firm fibrin clot.

The third step is the formation of the fibrin clot generated from the circulating clotting proteins, which we call a scab when on the surface of the body.

Contrary to popular belief, outward bleeding from a wound does not disable most hemophiliacs; rather internal bleeding does. Bleeding beneath the surface of the skin that is manifested by discoloration and swelling can be fatal.

One of the major problems faced by people with hemophilia is recurrent joint bleeds. The joints involved are the larger weight-bearing joints like the knees, hips, shoulders, and elbows. Ordinary daily use subjects these joints to relatively heavy trauma. Consider the fact that a person who weighs 150 pounds exerts a pressure of 472 pounds per square inch on the joint between the upper and lower leg when the knee is bent to an angle of 30 degrees. These everyday pressures cause small bleeding points in all people. Most of us are unaware of them. However, the hemophiliac will continue to bleed into the joint until it becomes painful and swollen. Repeated bleeds will result in the joint becoming brittle and the joint lining thickened. Recurrent bleeding into the joint causes extensive destruction of the smooth white cartilage lining of the joint. Often degenerative arthritis sets in.

When bleeding occurs on the surface, it is easily recognized and quickly treated. When injuries occur to deep tissues or organ systems, symptoms of internal bleeding can be more subtle and difficult to recognize.

TREATMENT

Clotting factor concentrates are now readily available to replace the deficient Factor VIII and Factor XI. People with bleeding disorders can be taught to administer the substance at home, thereby providing immediate treatment for suspected bleeding problems.

EFFECT ON LIFESTYLE

A person with hemophilia will tend to bruise easily, have swollen joints, and experience considerable limitation of movement. There may be intense pain in the joints. Hemophiliacs should not be involved in any form of contact sport. Aspirin and aspirin-containing drugs should be avoided because of their interference with platelet function. Hemophilia itself should not affect the expected life span. However, because people with bleeding disorders frequently require blood transfusions, acquired immune deficiency syndrome has now become the leading cause of death among hemophiliacs.

APPEARANCE

Other than wearing a "Medic Alert" bracelet, the person with a bleeding disorder will not be recognizable in the community.

RESOURCE

National Hemophilia Foundation
25 West 39th Street
New York, NY 10018

HUNTINGTON'S CHOREA

Classification: Illness

Huntington's chorea affects a total of about 25,000 people in the United States. It indirectly affects an additional 100,000 of their blood relatives who live with the possibility that they, too, might develop the disease.

Huntington's chorea is a degenerative brain disorder that causes progressive and irreversible deterioration of mental function and movement. The end result of the disease, after several years of intense suffering for both the person and the family, is death.

The cause of the condition is a defective gene that results in a premature degeneration of brain cells deep in the center of the brain where movement is coordinated. The cells of the brain's outer surface that control the functions of thought, perception, and memory are also affected. The damaging results of this defective gene usually surface between the ages of thirty-five and forty-five, but people both older and younger are not always exempt from the onset of symptoms. Those who develop the disease between the ages of four and nineteen exhibit a rapid degeneration, whereas those who develop the symptoms later in life generally experience slower degeneration. The slow, progressive decline to death usually takes around seventeen years.

Huntington's chorea is inherited as an autosomal dominant genetic trait, which means that everyone who carries the gene develops the disease. An affected parent can pass the condition on to his or her children. Because each parent contributes one of two genes to their offspring, the child has a 50 percent chance of inheriting the gene and developing the disease. By the time symptoms appear, most people have completed their childbearing and may have transmitted the gene to another generation.

The first symtpoms of Huntington's chorea are usually dismissed as normal variations in mood and behavior or are attributed to other causes. Complaints of depression, irritability, clumsiness, and slowing down are difficult to use as precise diagnostic tools for people who have no family history of the condition.

New developments in diagnostic technology have made it possible, in some families, to test members for the presence of the defective gene before they develop symptoms. It is also possible to test fetuses. However, the test requires a blood sample from the family member who has Huntington's in order to identify the DNA marker for the gene specific to that particular family.

TREATMENT

At present there is no effective therapy to prevent, treat, or cure this condition.

EFFECT ON LIFESTYLE

During the lengthy span of Huntington's chorea, progressively worsening symptoms run the gamut from uncontrollable muscle spasms to mental incompetence. Ultimately the disease will confine the person to a wheelchair and then to bed, where they are unaware of their surroundings until death.

Compounding the tragedy is the long-endured emotional and financial burden to the person's loved ones, some of whom may be at risk themselves and must witness their future fate.

There is some difference between the behavior exhibited by men and women with the condition. Men have a greater tendency to angry outbursts of temper than do women. Women become seriously depressed more often than men. The disease progression is often more rapid for women. People who inherit the gene from their father tend to decline more rapidly than those who get it from their mother.

The genetic test for Huntington's chorea is over 99 percent accurate, which creates an unusual dilemma for people who may be at risk. Each person must decide if it is best to know the future and perhaps not marry or have children, or to live life simply hoping for the best as most of us do.

ACCOMMODATION

The first thing that needs to be dealt with is the fear and depression that a person experiences after hearing the diagnosis of Huntington's chorea. Support from a trained counselor or psychotherapist may be required.

At some point in the progression of the disease, the person will no longer be able to maintain his or her place in society and will be cared for in the home or in an institution. The time at which this happens depends on how fast the person deteriorates and the tolerance of others.

RESOURCE

National Institute of Neurological and Communicative Disorders and Stroke (NINDS)
Building 31, Room 8A16

National Institutes of Health
Bethesda, MD 20892
(301) 496-5751

KLINEFELTER'S SYNDROME

Classification: Birth Defect

This birth defect is a genetic endocrine disorder that affects one in every five hundred males. Its cause is an extra X chromosome. Normal males have the XY chromosome type, but males born with this syndrome have an XXY chromosome structure (see Figure 3).

Figure 3
The Etiology of Klinefelter's Syndrome

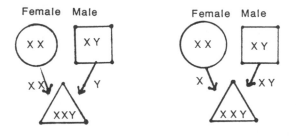

Normally, each parent contributes one sex chromosome to the fetus. In the case of a male with Klinefelter's syndrome, one parent contributes two sex chromosomes, resulting in a male child with the XXY genetic makeup.

Klinefelter's syndrome is probably the most common single cause of sexual underdevelopment and infertility in humans.

The penis and scrotum appear normal, and the condition may remain unrecognized until puberty. At puberty there is incomplete masculinization, the testes remain abnormally small, and there is a decrease in male sex hormone production. Body and pubic hair are sparse. An estimated 50 percent of men who have Klinefelter's syndrome develop some female characteristics, such as enlarged breasts.

Compared to normal males, people with this condition have a slightly greater incidence of physical disorders, including heart, hearing, and dental abnormalities. Neurological development can be delayed, resulting in problems with coordination, speed, dexterity, and strength. There is also a variety of psychological problems, including social maladjustment, emotional disturbances, high stress anxiety, immaturity, and alcoholism. Approximately 15 percent of those with the condition have below-average intelligence; those with normal intelligence often have learning disabilities and may be passive and poorly motivated. Life expectancy is entirely normal.

TREATMENT

Prenatal diagnosis is possible by analyzing the chromosomal nature of fetal cells gathered by amniocentesis. Early diagnosis and treatment with testosterone can decrease the effects of the disorder. Psychological and educational support are also required to achieve the best results.

EFFECT ON LIFESTYLE

Men with Klinefelter's syndrome often demonstrate underachievement, aggressiveness, withdrawal, immaturity, apathy, and poor relationships with their peers. Breast tissue in affected men has a risk for developing cancer that is twenty times greater than males in the general population. A man born with Klinefelter's syndrome is infertile.

APPEARANCE

Men with this condition tend to be tall, with very long legs. Muscles fail to develop fully and the voice may remain high-pitched. The distribution of fat on the body may give them a somewhat feminine shape.

ACCOMMODATION

No accommodation is required for the person who has Klinefelter's syndrome.

RESOURCES

There are no known organizations for men with Klinefelter's syndrome. A physician who specializes in reproductive medicine should be consulted for further information.

LUPUS
(Systemic Lupus Erythematosus)

Classification: Illness

More than half a million people in the United States have lupus, and approximately 16,000 new cases are diagnosed each year. Nearly 95 percent of lupus patients between the ages of 13 and 40 are female. However, in the over- 40 age group the ratio of male to female is nearly 50-50. Lupus can occur at any age, and it affects all racial and ethnic groups. It is approximately three times more common among black people than white people.

Lupus is a chronic illness but is not always fatal. Nearly 90 percent of people with lupus live at least ten years after developing the disease.

Systemic lupus erythematosus is a chronic inflammatory disease of connective tissue, which affects the skin, joints, heart, kidneys, circulatory system, nervous system, and mucous membranes—virtually every organ in the body. Though the exact cause of the condition is unknown, it is thought to be an autoimmune disorder.

People with lupus build an unusually high number of antibodies, which become abnormal and begin to attack healthy tissue. In a sense, the body becomes allergic to itself. When the antibodies attack an area, it becomes inflamed and tissue damage results. This tissue damage can occur in two ways: antibodies can attack and damage tissue directly, or antibodies can cause inflammation that in turn damages tissue.

There are two main types of lupus: discoid lupus and systemic lupus. Discoid lupus affects only the skin. This form of the illness is characterized by patchy disc-shaped reddened areas that appear on the scalp, face, neck, and upper chest. It can be painful and may result in scarring. Systemic lupus affects the internal organs, and it can be very severe if it affects vital organs. Systemic lupus can also affect the skin. Both forms of the illness feature episodic exacerbations, or flares. Flare-ups can often be controlled with medication. Occasionally symptoms will almost disappear for sustained periods.

TREATMENT

The goal of treatment is to suppress the symptoms of the disease. Anti-inflammatory medications are used to reduce inflammation and thus tissue damage. Steroids and immunosuppressant drugs are used only in the most severe cases. The effectiveness of plasmapheresis is being evaluated for people with lupus. In plasmapheresis the blood is separated into two components: plasma and blood cells. Then person's plasma is then replaced with an artificial plasma. This process removes antibodies in the blood. There is no cure for lupus at the present.

EFFECT ON LIFESTYLE

Every case of lupus is unique—with different symptoms and effects.

Persons with discoid lupus should avoid direct sunlight. The skin will tend to bruise easily, and hair loss is common. Many people with this form of the illness also have Raynaud's phenomenon, in which the skin of the fingers and toes turns bluish or white from lack of circulation.

If the chest is involved, there may be difficulty in breathing, shortness of breath, pain from inflammation of the membranes around the heart and lungs, or rapid heart rate. Joint pain is very common. When the blood is involved, people may be anemic, or they may have very high or very low white blood counts. Lupus patients may also have a false positive result on tests for syphilis. Stomach pain, cramps, nausea, vomiting, diarrhea, or constipation are common for people whose digestive system is involved.

One of the most serious aspects of lupus is the possibility of kidney disease. About 50 percent of people with lupus develop some degree of kidney inflammation, and of them about 5 percent will eventually need dialysis or a kidney transplant.

People who have nervous system involvement may experience head-aches, seizures, or temporary paralysis. Cognitive difficulties occur in as many as 75 percent of cases at some time during the illness. Episodes of psychotic behavior can occur.

ACCOMMODATION

The accommodation required will depend on the type of lupus present and the extent of involvement. The best source of help in this area is the person who is affected.

RESOURCES

Lupus Foundation of America, Inc.
4 Research Place, Suite 180
Rockville, MD 20850-3226

American Lupus Society
23751 Madison Street
Torrance, CA 90505
(213) 373-1335

MARFAN'S SYNDROME

Classification: Birth Defect

Marfan's syndrome results from a single abnormal gene present at birth, though the syndrome may be diagnosed at any age. Marfan's is believed to affect more than forty thousand Americans at the present time. It affects males and females equally and knows no ethnic borders. Although there is no cure for the condition, there are effective treatments, and most people affected will live normal, active lives.

Marfan's syndrome is an inherited disorder of the connective tissue (material that holds tissues of the body together) characterized by excessive height, particularly long limbs (which are thin, loose-jointed, and long in relation to the torso) and long slender fingers and toes; the spine may have scoliosis; the breastbone may protrude or look caved in; the roof of the mouth is high; the teeth may be crowded; and the face will be long and thin. Internal signs of Marfan's syndrome are oversized and floppy heart valves, which allow brief reverse blood flow during heart-beats, and/or a defective aortic artery. The lens of one eye is off-center in 50 percent of those affected. People with Marfan's are more prone to lung collapse than the general population. All of the possible signs and symptoms rarely appear together in one person.

Mitral and aortic heart valves control the flow of blood through the heart. Defects of the mitral valve may cause shortness of breath, an irregular pulse, and undue tiredness. Aortic valve defects can lead to heart failure. If the aortic artery is defective it can become weakened and may rupture. Rupture of the aorta has been the cause of sudden death in some people who did not know they had Marfan's syndrome.

Marfan's syndrome does not affect intelligence.

TREATMENT

Those aware of having Marfan's syndrome may seek treatment for some of the internal problems, such as heart surgery to repair or replace defective valves. However, there is no treatment for the condition itself.

EFFECT ON LIFESTYLE

Excessive height is not a serious medical concern, but can cause a child to become self-conscious and withdrawn. In addition, because they are taller than children of the same age they are often expected to act more maturely. The self-perception of the child becomes the self-perception of the adult.

When the eyes are affected, nearsightedness is a common condition. The lens of the eye (which is the focusing apparatus) can become torn from its supports. This can cause vision problems severe enough to interfere with schooling. If the retina of the eye becomes detached, it will cause sudden loss of vision and require emergency surgery.

Infections develop easily in defective heart valves; therefore, antibiotics are usually required before and after any surgery including such things as tooth extractions and routine dental care.

Pregnancy and childbirth put an extra strain on a woman's heart. Women with Marfan's syndrome should discuss the implications of the condition with their doctors before pregnancy.

Any sports activity that may involve a blow to the face (football, racquetball, boxing, diving, etc.) should be avoided by those people whose eyes are affected. People who have suspected heart involvement should avoid strenuous activities such as track, basketball, baseball, or football. In the work environment, heavy lifting can cause excessive heart strain and should be avoided.

APPEARANCE

A person with Marfan's syndrome will have very long legs and arms with a normal-length torso. The lens of one eye may be off-center, and the person may wear glasses. Otherwise, there will be no visible indication of disability. Abraham Lincoln is thought to have had Marfan's syndrome.

ACCOMMODATION

There are no structural accommodations that need to be made for the person with Marfan's syndrome. Strenuous activity, including heavy lifting, should be eliminated.

RESOURCES

The Arthritis Foundation
1212 Avenue of the Americas
New York, NY 10036

The National Foundation/March of Dimes
1275 Mamaroneck Avenue
White Plains, NY 10605

National Marfan Foundation
382 Main Street
Port Washington, NY 10050

MULTIPLE SCLEROSIS

Classification: Illness

Multiple sclerosis is a disease of the myelin sheath that insulates and envelops the nerves in the brain and spinal column. The illness derives its name from the fact that many scattered areas of the brain and spinal cord are affected by sclerosed or hardened patches of scar tissue that form over damaged myelin.

Each year approximately eight thousand Americans are diagnosed with multiple sclerosis. Because the symptoms associated with multiple sclerosis vary markedly from person to person and often change in an individual, diagnosing multiple sclerosis is not an easy task. No absolutely specific diagnostic tests are yet available.

The cause of multiple sclerosis is unknown, but the results of the illness are well understood.

Multiple sclerosis occurs in genetically susceptible people, usually between the ages of twenty and fifty (it has been seen as late as the mid-sixties and as early as childhood). It is more common in women than in men. The disease is unusual in Orientals, unknown in African blacks, and less frequent in American blacks. People of Germanic, Anglo-Saxon, and Scandinavian origin appear to be more prone to this disease. It is more common in countries farther from the equator, in both the northern and southern hemispheres.

The nerves of the human body can be compared to electric cords. An impulse is generated at one end of the cord and travels along the wire to the other end, where it causes an action. The wires are surrounded with an insulating material that prevents the electricity from leaking out. In the human body the material insulating the nerves is called myelin (see Figure 4). When the myelin is damaged, the nerve impulse "leaks" from the nerve and results in either delayed transmission or no transmission at all. Scar tissue forms wherever the myelin is damaged; however, this hardened tissue does not have the insulating ability of myelin and also

Figure 4
Structure of a Motor Neuron

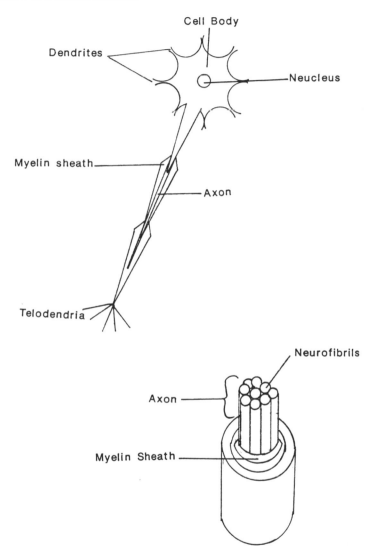

Cell Body

Dendrites

Neucleus

Myelin sheath

Axon

Telodendria

Neurofibrils

Axon

Myelin Sheath

prevents myelin regrowth. The result is diminished or lost nervous system activity.

The symptoms of multiple sclerosis vary according to which nerves have myelin damage, and, because there are so many different nerves to serve different parts of the body, some people are affected only in one area while others have generalized difficulty.

The more common symptoms of multiple sclerosis are weakness, numbness, tingling, loss of balance and coordination, fatigue, dizziness, impotence, muscle spasms, slurring of speech, burning or sensations of pain, blind spots in the center of vision, blurred or double vision, and in severe cases, loss of bowel and bladder control.

Multiple sclerosis is rarely fatal. The average life expectancy is reduced, however, to 93 percent of that of the general population. The disease is not always disabling. Some people have only one attack, with no worsening or spreading of symptoms thereafter. Two-thirds of patients are still able to walk (with or without help) twenty-five years after their disease was first diagnosed. Many can still engage in the activities they enjoyed before developing the illness for as long as twenty years after its onset.

There are four basic types of multiple sclerosis:

Benign—seen in 20 percent of patients and characterized by few attacks and complete or near-complete remission. The symptoms tend to involve sensory or visual nerves.

Relapsing/remitting—seen in 25 percent of patients, and similar to benign except that attacks are worse and tend to involve more of the body.

Relapsing/progressive—seen in 40 percent of patients and characterized by serious attacks with incomplete recovery.

Progressive—seen in about 15 percent and characterized by a slowly progressive decline, rather than an attack pattern, with no remission or recovery. People with this type of multiple sclerosis tend to have severe disability within a few years of diagnosis.

TREATMENT

Since the cause of multiple sclerosis is not known, there is no treatment that will prevent it, lessen it, or cure it. Symptomatic and rehabilitative treatments are the most effective approaches and fall into four general categories:

Pharmacological—use of drugs
Surgical—cutting nerves or tendons, etc.
Physical—exercise, massage, heat, etc.
Psychological—counseling or group support

A variety of drugs may be used to relieve the stiffness, loss of balance, spasticity, and other motor disabilities. These drugs are used for brief periods, almost never more than one month. When a person is incapacitated by fatigue caused by the illness, there are medications that can be used safely.

Surgery is only rarely used and when it is, it is generally done to facilitate motion rather than as a curative measure.

Physical therapy and exercise are most effective when used during recovery from an attack. The goal is to increase strength and endurance and to maintain the ability to walk.

Psychological counseling and group support are important to the patient and to family members who are dealing with euphoria or depression.

EFFECT ON LIFESTYLE

The symptoms of multiple sclerosis can come and go mysteriously in the beginning stages of the illness. As the disease progresses, the attacks become more frequent and there is less remission, until in the late stages there is a progressive decline with no remissions.

People with multiple sclerosis can have changes in some facets of intellectual functioning. Around half of those people with multiple sclerosis have no evidence at all of cognitive changes. Of the other half, less than 10 percent have moderate to severe dysfunction.

A person with multiple sclerosis may have difficulty walking because of weakness in the legs, stiffness, imbalance, or a combination of these problems. Often there is difficulty in walking over rough surfaces like carpets, pebbled walkways, or unpaved areas. There can be difficulty climbing stairs or stepping over curbs. Frequently there is an inability to balance while walking, causing the person to walk with feet spread wide apart.

If the arms are weak or tremble, there will be difficulty with fine finger movements and lifting or holding things.

Reduced vision, blurring, double vision, and sometimes loss of vision in one eye are frequently a problem. However, blindness or persistent loss of vision is uncommon.

Urgency, frequency, incontinence, or inability to empty the bladder are common problems associated with the disease. Equally common are bowel function problems such as constipation, urgency, or incontinence.

Failure to achieve erection or impotence in men and inability to achieve orgasm in females are problems associated with multiple sclerosis. It is not clear whether the cause is neurological (loss of sensation) or psychological.

APPEARANCE

It is important to remember that the appearance of people with multiple sclerosis can and will change from day to day, depending on whether they are experiencing an attack or are in a remission and also depending on which of the nerves is involved. There will be good days and bad days.

A shuffling gait or dragging one foot is common with multiple sclerosis. Speech may sound slurred, similar to one who has had too much alcohol. There may be tremors when initiating motion, but not when the limb is at rest. There is no reason to expect any visible anatomical changes or any displeasing appearance or habits in a person who has multiple sclerosis.

ACCOMMODATION

There are limitless ways for multiple sclerosis to affect a person. For this reason, accommodations can range from none at all to major changes. The best source for information is the person who is affected.

The following is a partial list of accommodations that have been used successfully:

Dictating machines when writing is difficult

Battery-powered handtools for weakness

Handrails where the walking surface is uneven

Workstation moved closer to the restroom

Flexible work schedule

Computer customized to the individual's need

Book rests to hold reference material

Ramps for wheelchair or scooter users

RESOURCES

National Multiple Sclerosis Society
205 East 42nd Street
New York, NY 10017

Multiple Sclerosis Society of Canada
250 Bloor Street East, Suite 820
Toronto, Ontario M4W3P9
Canada

Multiple Sclerosis Society of Great Britain and North Ireland
25 Effie Road
London SW61EE
United Kingdom

MUSCULAR DYSTROPHY

Classification: Birth Defect

Muscular dystrophy is a general term for a group of hereditary diseases characterized by progressive wasting of voluntary muscles without any evidence of neural tissue involvement. There are five primary forms of muscular dystrophy (myotonic, Duchenne, Becker, limb-girdle, facioscapulohumeral), all differing only in severity, age of onset, rate of progression, and the muscles affected. One out of every five hundred children has, or will get, muscular dystrophy.

A muscle cell makes ten thousand different proteins during its lifetime, each of which has an exact function in the normal growth and development of a muscle. Genes are the body's blueprints for production and are found in every cell of the body. A defect in a single gene that impairs the production of just one of these ten thousand proteins can cause muscular dystrophy. The affected muscle group will become weaker and weaker over time. Exercise will not make the muscles strong. This genetic defect is passed from parent to child by one of three inheritance patterns: dominant, recessive, or sex-linked (see Figure 5).

Myotonic Dystrophy

This form of muscular dystrophy is the most common adult form. It has a dominant inheritance pattern; therefore, it affects both sexes equally. The illness is generally manifested by stiffness in the hands and feet, especially after a chill, and difficulty relaxing a grip. Facial muscles may be affected, causing drooping eyelids and inability to keep the jaw closed. Frequent tripping and falling are common. The symptoms usually appear in young adults but occasionally show up as early as adolescence. The weakening effect spreads steadily until walking becomes difficult. In addition to the primary muscles affected, myotonic dystrophy can affect the tissues and organs of many other body systems. Severe disability usually results after a period of ten to fifteen years. Lifespan is generally shortened.

Figure 5
Inheritance Patterns of Muscular Dystrophy

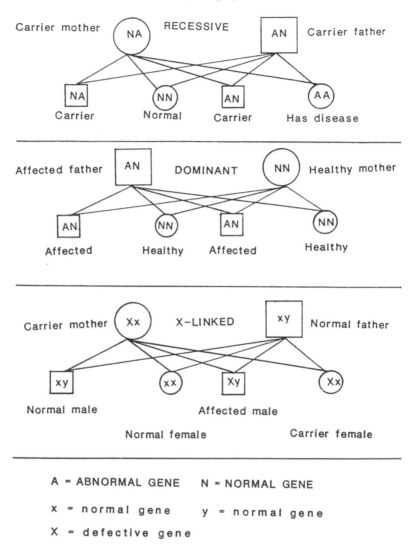

A = ABNORMAL GENE   N = NORMAL GENE

x = normal gene   y = normal gene

X = defective gene

Duchenne Dystrophy

This form of dystrophy (sometimes called pseudohypertrophic dystrophy) is sex-linked recessive and affects only boys. It is the most common and most severe childhood form, usually manifesting itself between the ages of two and six. Weakness begins in the large muscles of the lower trunk and upper legs, affecting the ability to walk. The disease progresses rapidly; generally by the age of twelve the child will need a wheelchair. During the latter stages, breathing becomes affected, leading to frequent respiratory infections that usually claim the person's life in the mid-twenties.

Becker Muscular Dystrophy

This form is very similar to Duchenne, but starts later in life, even as late as age twenty-five, and is less severe. The progression is usually slower and allows a longer life expectancy.

Limb-Girdle Dystrophy

This form of muscular dystrophy is inherited in the recessive pattern and can affect either sex. The symptoms usually become obvious in late childhood or early adolescence. When the affected muscles are in the shoulder, symptoms are manifested as difficulty raising the arms or lifting objects. If the muscles affected are in the lower trunk and upper legs, the symptoms are a waddling gait, frequent falls with difficulty rising from the floor, and difficulty climbing stairs. This disease seems to progress slower if it begins in the shoulder muscles and more rapidly if it begins in the lower trunk. Most people become severely disabled and need to use a wheelchair by middle age. Respiratory function and heart muscles may be affected; if so, the disease can shorten life expectancy.

Facioscapulohumeral Muscular Dystrophy

There is usually a strong family history of this form of dystrophy because it is transmitted as a dominant gene. Symptoms generally become evident in the teen years, but may appear at any age. The muscles affected are in the face (facio), manifested by difficulty closing the eyes and whistling; shoulders (scapulo), manifested by forward sloping shoulders and pronounced shoulder blades; and upper arms (humeral), manifested by difficulty raising the arms or difficulty lifting things.

Progress of this condition is often very slow, with long periods when symptoms don't get worse. Occasionally, there is rapid progression of the disease with trunk and leg muscles becoming involved. If a wheelchair becomes necessary, it will be a motorized type because weakness in the arms precludes the self-propelled kind. Life span is often normal.

TREATMENT

At present there is no cure for any of the muscular dystrophies and no treatment that will stop its course. Exercise programs and physical therapy can help keep muscles as flexible as possible. Mobility aids, ranging from canes to electric wheelchairs, help maintain independence as long as possible.

EFFECT ON LIFESTYLE

The muscular dystrophies can have a wide range of effects depending on the specific type and severity of the illness. Some of the more common problems include limited range of motion, inability to walk, difficulty opening or closing the eyelids, frequent falls, stiffening of muscles after use, difficulty breathing, difficulty swallowing, heart problems, and general weakness. If the condition is severe, the person may need help with the activities of daily living. There is no loss of bowel or bladder control.

APPEARANCE

There should be no abnormalities, other than those associated with weak muscles. A person who has facioscapulohumeral dystrophy will have an unlined face, even in middle age. Early in the disease process of myotonic dystrophy weakness of facial, jaw, and neck muscles will be apparent, as will frontal balding in men. If serious deformities or missing limbs are present, the person is dealing with other conditions as well as muscular dystrophy.

ACCOMMODATION

Adjustments will need to be made for weak muscles in everything from how a phone is answered to how a person moves from place to place. A speaker phone will eliminate the need to hold the receiver. Doors will need to open automatically or have minimum pull required. Wheelchair access may be necessary. Each accommodation will be specific to the person affected.

RESOURCE

Muscular Dystrophy Association
810 Seventh Avenue, Twenty-Seventh Floor
New York, NY 10019

MYASTHENIA GRAVIS

Classification: Illness

Myasthenia affects approximately one in 15,000 persons and is, therefore, a relatively rare illness. The age of onset is usually between twenty and thirty years for women and forty to sixty years for men. Almost twice as many women are affected as men.

Myasthenia gravis comes from the Greek words for "grave muscle weakness." The distinctive feature of myasthenia gravis is fluctuating weakness of certain voluntary muscles, made worse by use and sometimes improved by resting the muscles involved. The muscles used for facial expression, smiling, chewing, talking, swallowing, seeing, and even keeping the eyelids open can be affected as well as those for breathing or moving the arms and legs. Muscles that are not affected include the heart and smooth muscles of the intestine and uterus. Skin sensations remain normal.

The voluntary muscles of the body are controlled by nerve impulses originating in the brain. These impulses move down the nerves to the place where the nerve meets the muscle fibers. There is a space between where the nerve ends and the muscle fiber begins called the neuromuscular junction. When the impulse reaches the end of the nerve, it releases a chemical that travels across that space to the muscle fiber side of the junction. There are many receptors on each muscle fiber and when enough of the receptors have received the chemical, the muscle will contract.

The immune system of the person with myasthenia gravis makes antibodies against the receptor sites and destroys them more rapidly than they can be replaced by the body. As many as 80 percent of the receptors can be destroyed, which would reduce muscle strength to 20 percent of normal.

Most people have a gradual onset of myasthenia. For others, there is a rapid onset, especially if it follows an illness, trauma, or emotional upset. Stress always makes the symptoms worse and can cause severe muscle weakness in a very short time.

Different muscle groups are affected in different people with myasthenia gravis. Some have ocular myasthenia, which involves only the eye muscles and eyelids; others have difficulty swallowing and talking; some have generalized problems affecting many muscle groups. The maximum number of muscles involved will display itself within the first few years and will not increase thereafter, even though muscle strength and involvement will fluctuate from day to day.

TREATMENT

There are several treatments for myasthenia gravis, each having good results for some and none for others; therefore, medication types and schedules will vary considerably. There is no cure at the present time.

EFFECT ON LIFESTYLE

When respiratory muscles are affected, the person will have difficulty breathing, which can become severe enough and develop quickly enough to create a crisis. Ineffective breathing is a medical emergency requiring immediate medical attention. Some people with respiratory involvement will use a spirometer for home breathing evaluation and gauge their activity accordingly.

The inability to swallow can be a constant concern for people with myasthenia. In addition to presenting problems with nutrition, the potential for aspiration of food or saliva is very real. If the airway is blocked by food, they may not have the usual reserve strength for coughing repetitively and strongly enough to dislodge the blockage. It may be necessary for people with this involvement to switch to soft foods when swallowing is difficult.

Eye muscles seem to be involved more often than any other muscle group. Most people with myasthenia have trouble moving their eyes and eyelids. They may appear sleepy because of the inability to keep the eyelids open and may experience double vision because of the inability to focus properly.

When facial muscles are involved, it is common to have difficulty creating appropriate facial expressions. A snarl may replace a smile because of muscle weakness.

The muscles used for speaking are the same as those used for chewing. Persons with weakness in this area will experience problems with both eating and talking. Speech may sound as if the person is intoxicated. It may be necessary to cut food into very tiny portions or change to a soft diet.

Fatigue in other muscles used in daily living is a problem for most people with myasthenia. They may have trouble holding up their heads because of weak neck muscles. Many will not be able to hold their arms up or will have trouble getting out of a chair or climbing stairs. Walking, lifting, and sitting can all be exhausting for a person with myasthenia gravis.

Prolonged exposure to heat or cold may increase symptoms in some people. Women may have increased difficulty during menses and pregnancy.

In some cases, myasthenia gravis will go into remission, which can last many years. During these periods, muscle weakness disappears and treatment may not be necessary.

APPEARANCE

If muscles that control breathing are affected, breathing will be shallow and will preclude any strenuous efforts. When muscles of the eyes are affected, the person may have to wear an eye patch to rest muscles of the eye. The patch will be worn alternately on each eye. It is often difficult for this person to focus the eyes, so double vision is often a problem. People with ocular myasthenia have been known to use tape or eyelid "crutches" to keep their eyelids open. People with generalized myasthenia may have an overall fatigued apperance.

ACCOMMODATION

People with myasthenia gravis may find it necessary to alter their work or school schedule in order to remain active without undue stress. This can include working only part-time, flexible hours, or light assignments.

The following suggestions should be implemented whenever possible:

Myasthenics should never stand when they can sit.

Schedule regular rest periods during each day.

Move frequently used items to easily accessible places.

Use power tools when possible.

Avoid aerosol pesticides and cleaners (many contain neuromuscular paralyzing agents and may adversely affect the person with myasthenia).

Avoid stressful situations.

RESOURCE

Myasthenia Gravis Foundation
53 West Jackson Boulevard, Suite 1352
Chicago, IL 60604

NEUROFIBROMATOSIS

Classification: Birth Defect

Neurofibromatosis, also known as multiple neuroma, neuromatosis, and von Recklinghausen's disease, is an inherited genetic disease that occurs in one out of every 2,500 births. It occurs in every racial and ethnic group throughout the world and affects males and females alike.

The condition can be inherited from a parent who carries the gene, or it can be the result of a spontaneous mutation of the individual gene. Regardless of whether the condition is spontaneous or the result of inheritance, the children of people who have neurofibromatosis have a 50-50 chance of inheriting the gene.

Children with this condition are usually identified shortly after birth by the presence of five or more "cafe-au-lait" spots, of half a centimeter or more in diameter, anywhere on the body. The spots may increase in size and number as the child matures and may also become somewhat darker.

During adolescence, but occasionally in early childhood or as late as fifty years old, small benign tumors develop in the body. These tumors are made up of nerve and other cell types and are located on the nerve trunks of the extremities as well as on the nerves of the head, neck, and body. Often some of the first tumors to be investigated are the tiny dark nodules that appear on the iris. These tiny tumors do not affect vision, but help to verify the illness.

Neurofibromatosis has been divided into two types, though each has some characteristics of the other.

Peripheral neurofibromatosis has the usual cafe-au-lait spots, a number of small tumors, and a network of larger tumors under the skin. The bones and other body parts can become enlarged and deformed. Left-right curvature of the spine is common. Tumors sometimes develop in the brain, on the cranial nerves, or on the spinal cord.

Central neurofibromatosis with bilateral acoustic neuromas is characterized by tumors of both auditory nerves that cause deafness beginning at about twenty years of age. Tumors may grow on the optic nerves and cause blindness. Multiple tumors on the cranial and spinal nerves and other lesions of the brain and spinal cord are part of this condition.

TREATMENT

There is no treatment for this disease. However, surgical removal of tumors located in the brain or spine is possible. When this is done, there is danger that the tumors will grow back in even greater numbers. Cosmetic surgery for painful, disfiguring, or disabling growths is also possible, but these too may grow back. Curvature of the spine can be treated with surgery, a brace, or both.

EFFECT ON LIFESTYLE

The drastic deformity represented by "The Elephant Man" is extremely rare; however, there is no way of predicting the degree of disability this condition will cause. In most cases the symptoms are mild and people live a normal life.

Many children with neurofibromatosis have learning disabilities and some may be overactive. The extent of neurological impairment is entirely random and depends on whether or not there are brain tumors, their number, and their location.

Finding attractive, well-fitting clothing can be a problem. Often if the condition is severe the person will opt for baggy, loose-fitting apparel. When there are large or numerous tumors on the feet, shoes will not fit properly.

The most common problems faced by people with this condition are psychological. Because they feel different and sometimes ugly, many people become lonely and withdrawn. There is a 3 to 5 percent chance that one or more of these tumors may become malignant. Many people with this condition are worried about passing the gene to their children.

If there are bone deformities, mobility and range of motion may be a problem. Spinal deformitites are common.

APPEARANCE

The person with neurofibromatosis has numerous lumps under the skin, which may or may not be evident to the casual observer. Large tumors are usually evident regardless of their location on the body. If they are on the face or hands, even small tumors can be cosmetically unappealing. In spite of surgical intervention, the spine may be curved and other skeletal abnormalities may also be present. The person may be deaf, blind, or both.

ACCOMMODATION

The most important accommodation is an accepting attitude. The disfiguring nature of this condition makes most people who have it very self-conscious and withdrawn. Peers need to be assured that it is not contagious and encouraged to make a sincere offer of friendship.

If the person has a mobility impairment or sensory impairment—blindness or deafness—accommodations for these conditions need to be made based on the impairment itself with no special emphasis on the cause.

RESOURCES

The National Neurofibromatosis Foundation, Inc.
70 West 40th Street
New York, NY 10018
(212) 869-9034

Neurofibromatosis Clinic
Inter-Institute Genetics Program
Building 10, Room 1D21
National Institutes of Health
Bethesda, MD 20205
(301) 496-1380

OSTEOGENESIS IMPERFECTA

Classification: Birth Defect

Osteogenesis imperfecta, often called "brittle bone disease," is a condition in which the bones are weak in structure. In addition, all of the collagen in the tissues is immature, resulting in greater flexibility in the joints and skin.

There are two forms of this condition: congenital osteogenesis imperfecta, which occurs in one out of 50,000 births; and osteogenesis imperfecta tarda, which occurs in one out of 25,000 births. Males and females are equally affected, and there is no indication of racial predominance.

The difference between the congenital and tarda forms of the condition is that babies born with the congenital type may have broken bones at birth and may not even survive the birth process. Babies born with the tarda form do not exhibit the weakness until some time after birth.

The basic defect appears to be in the protein makeup of the bones, which remain very similar to bone in a developing fetus—entirely immature.

By the time most children are seven or eight years old, they are wheelchair users because the simple act of putting weight on leg bones occurs often enough to break them. During late adolescence the condition usually arrests itself and bones are no longer so fragile.

It is not unusual for a person to reach the age of fifteen having had more than fifty fractures. Therefore, the extent of damage is enormous and irreversible.

TREATMENT

Leg bracing, sometimes including surgery to insert metal rods into leg bones for support, and a comprehensive rehabilitation program can result in a high level of functional activity for someone with osteogenesis imperfecta. There is no cure for the condition.

EFFECT ON LIFESTYLE

The condition generally requires people to use a wheelchair, perhaps throughout their entire life due to fractures that did not heal properly. Hearing loss is common in people with this condition, due to problems with the bones of the inner ear. Children born with osteogenesis imperfecta will grow into adults who have at least some deformities, the extent of which will depend on the number and nature of injuries sustained in childhood.

One of the problems associated with children who have an unusual number of broken bones is the potential for mistaking the injuries as evidence of child abuse. When abuse is suspected, a child is often removed from a familiar environment until the true situation is discovered. This adds further to the number of problems the child with osteogenesis imperfecta must face.

APPEARANCE

Most people with osteogenesis imperfecta have a very triangular face, broad forehead, and bulging temples. All the limbs are small and usually bowed in various ways due to repeated breaks. Generally the thigh bone bows outward, and the lower leg bows forward. The chest is barrel-shaped and the breast bone protrudes outward. The spine is rounded backward and is often curved.

ACCOMMODATION

Often the person with osteogenesis uses an electric wheelchair, which will require modification of things like the force needed to open doors, desk height, and workspace configuration. Computer setup may need to be adapted to specific abilities.

If the person has hearing impairment due to osteogenesis imperfecta, the accommodations for deafness will have to be made in addition to the physical accommodations.

The adult with osteogenesis imperfecta is no longer subject to easy bone fracture, so co-workers need not worry about everyday office contact. However, it is wise to avoid the "bone cruncher hand-shake" and keep rough-housing to the home front.

RESOURCES

National Easter Seal Society
2023 West Ogden Avenue
Chicago, IL 60612

March of Dimes
1275 Mamaroneck Avenue
White Plains, NY 10605

PARKINSON'S DISEASE

Classification: Illness

Between five hundred thousand and one million people in the United States have been diagnosed with Parkinson's disease. However, Parkinson's is not a disease in the true sense of the word. It is more accurate to describe it as a condition with a characteristic set of symptoms. The onset of these symptoms is most common in people about fifty-five years old. It is equally common in men and women.

The cause of Parkinson's is unknown, but the underlying dysfunction and its results are well understood. The source of the condition lies in the brain, in a system of nerve cells that look like freckles when seen by the naked eye. It is believed that these freckled areas produce and store a chemical messenger called dopamine, which sends signals to other parts of the brain. When there is a deficiency of dopamine, symptoms of Parkinson's disease begin to appear.

The chemical deficiency can have a number of causes: deterioration of the cells themselves, a brain tumor, a stroke, a virus that infects the brain, and certain drugs, to name just a few. The result of this chemical deficiency is a condition marked by a characteristic set of symptoms: tremor, muscular rigidity, slow movement (called "bradykinesia"), postural instability, and gait disturbance.

The onset of the symptoms of Parkinson's is gradual. Often the first signs are dismissed as signs of aging. Later, the person may have more specific complaints. However, because the symptoms of Parkinson's are also indicative of many other conditions, an accurate diagnosis is not generally made until three characteristic signs are present: tremor, rigidity, and bradykinesia. Even then a physician will have to rule out other illnesses.

TREATMENT

Although there is no cure for Parkinson's disease at the present time, there is evidence that treatment with certain drugs may retard progression of the disease if begun in the early stages. How the drugs actually work is not fully understood, and their effect is only partial. However, the symptoms of Parkinson's disease can be so well controlled that progression of the condition may be masked effectively for many years. Drug treatment will continue for the remainder of the person's life. Other symptoms of Parkinson's, such as insomnia, anxiety, and constipation, are treated individually as they arise.

EFFECT ON LIFESTYLE

The tremor apparent in Parkinson's is a resting tremor, which means that it appears when the affected area is at rest and disappears when it is in use. For some reason people are often embarrassed by this and try to hide the trembling from those around them. This trembling is not uniform or constant; sometimes it is pronounced and sometimes absent entirely.

A person who was once quick and vivacious may become slow and deliberate due to bradykinesia. The facial muscles may lose their ability to express emotions. One of the more obvious effects is difficulty in moving. There may be difficulty getting out of a car, getting up from a chair, turning over in bed, or getting dressed. Loss of balance makes people with Parkinson's very prone to falling—backward as well as forward.

People with Parkinson's may develop a monotonous voice, and speech may be inaudible or mumbled, with uncontrollable repetition of syllables. Rigid muscles may lead to eating and drooling problems.

When muscles that control the autonomic functions move slowly, or not at all, there will be problems with blood pressure, impotence, and constipation.

APPEARANCE

People with tremor often have a slow "pill-rolling" movement between the thumb and fingers that disappears when the hand is in use.

Rigid muscles make affected persons tend to move as a single unit—turning the head, shoulders, and trunk instead of just the head. They may not swing their arms when they walk. Bradykinesia will make them seem hesitant to begin movements. While walking they may freeze in place and appear as if their feet have been nailed to the floor, especially when they walk through a doorway or pivot to turn.

Don't misinterpret slow response as mental deficiency. True mental changes occur in only about 15 percent of those who have Parkinson's.

As the condition progresses, they may develop a stooped posture and an increased tendency to fall. Several gait problems may develop, such as the inability to stop after taking a step backward, or to ward off an impending fall they may break into a run of small rapid steps. The typical Parkinson's gait is shuffling and short-stepped and includes periods of walking in place with no forward progress.

It is not uncommon for every trace of Parkinson's to disappear for brief periods even in severely affected people. This does not mean they have been cured or that they did not really have the condition. It is simply a well-documented phenomenon whose mechanism is not understood. People will relapse to their former level of involvement, not to the beginning state.

ACCOMMODATION

Adaptive arrangements should include railings in hallways to aid with balance. Chairs should be firm with strong arms and should be relatively high. There are commercially available chairs with spring-loaded devices that may help some people with rising. Try them before buying, as some of these chairs have a catapult effect. Blocks under the legs of some chairs will raise the seats to a better height. Floor mats, especially rubber mats, will need to be removed to avoid tripping hazards. Speech amplification devices are sometimes useful for those whose voice is affected.

Consultation with an occupational therapist may be appropriate for those who need special instruction in such areas as dressing, attending to personal hygiene, and other activities.

RESOURCES

The Parkinson's Disease Foundation
William Black Medical Research Building
640 West 168th Street
New York, NY 10032

National Parkinson Foundation, Inc.
1501 Ninth Avenue, NW
Miami, FL 33136

The Parkinson Foundation of Canada
ManuLife Centre, Suite 232
55 Bloor Street, West
Toronto, Ontario M4W1A6
Canada

POLIO/POST-POLIO SYNDROME

Classification: Illness

Nearly 10 million people have some degree of disability caused by polio, and every year there are approximately two hundred thousand new cases worldwide. The World Health Organization estimates that 2 million more children will be affected by polio in the next ten years.

Polio, short for poliomyelitis, is an infectious disease caused by one of three different polioviruses. The disease occurs in three forms: asymptomatic, nonparalytic, and paralytic.

Asymptomatic infection has no obvious signs of illness, but it will give immunity to the other forms of the disease.

Nonparalytic poliomyelitis is characterized by severe pain and stiffness in the back, fever, malaise, headache, nausea, vomiting, and slight abdominal discomfort. The acute phase of the illness lasts only a few hours, after which the person recovers fully.

Paralytic polio begins the same as nonparalytic. After the symptoms fade, the person seems well for several days. Then the symptoms reappear and paralysis develops. The peak of paralysis is reached within the first week. The virus actively attacks the nerve cells for two weeks, but the person may carry the virus for up to six months after the acute phase of the illness.

The primary target of the infection is the motor nerve cells in the spinal cord, but cell damage occurs in the brain stem as well. Paralysis and weakness are greatest at the start of the illness when severe inflammation occurs in the spinal cord and the nerve cells. Some cells are only damaged, others are completely destroyed. The muscles controlled by the dead nerves begin to atrophy from lack of use; those muscles controlled by damaged nerves become very weak.

TREATMENT

Treatment for nonparalytic polio consists of bed rest, good diet, and for at least two weeks avoiding all types of overexertion, stress, or fatigue.

Paralytic polio treatment includes hospitalization, hot packs, range of motion exercises, and assisted breathing (the "iron lung") when necessary. As soon as the acute stage of the illness is over, comprehensive rehabilitation is promptly begun.

Deformities from polio can result from one of two things. First, if one muscle in a limb is paralyzed, but its opposing muscle is not, the strong muscle will pull the limb into an abnormal position. Second, completely paralyzed limbs that rest in one position tend to develop shortening of muscles and limitations in joint movement. In both cases, deformities can be prevented by having a therapist move the limbs through a range of positions each day.

Many survivors of paralytic polio have a recurrence of symptoms thirty or forty years after the initial infection. The post-polio syndrome is characterized by muscle fatigue, weakness, muscle pain, difficulty breathing, and an intolerance of cold. Many people also report difficulty swallowing.

Doctors are certain that post-polio syndrome is not a new infection, nor is it a reactivation of the old infection. However, what does cause the condition is a subject for debate. One widely held theory is that healthy nerve cells in the spinal cord give out after decades of taking over for nerve cells killed or damaged by the original polio infection. As a result, muscles that had been functional lose nerve stimulation and begin to atrophy. As many as 80 percent of polio survivors experience recurrence, and 5 percent of those have symptoms that are disabling enough to require a return to leg braces, a wheelchair, or even artificial ventilation.

TREATMENT

Painkillers and anti-inflammatory medications are the main treatments for post-polio syndrome when it is not severe. Severe cases require the same treatment as in the initial phase of the illness.

EFFECT ON LIFESTYLE

The effect of polio and post-polio syndrome depends on the severity of the initial infection and on the quality of rehabilitative care. Most people have some degree of ambulation, but may use braces, walkers, canes, and crutches. Those whose illness was severe may require a wheelchair. Even those whose initial illness was mild may have lasting muscle weakness.

People who have been diagnosed with polio or post-polio syndrome often have contractures or muscle shortening that causes pain and instability at related joints. Some lead sedentary lives, choosing not to exercise painful muscles. Breathing difficulties often impose restrictions on activity. Intolerance to cold and cold-induced weakness lead many people to warm climates or keeps them indoors in colder areas.

APPEARANCE

People with polio or post-polio will appear entirely normal, except that they may have weakened muscles that require braces or other support when they walk. Those who use wheelchairs will have nothing else that sets them apart.

The fact that the virus infected the brain stem does not interfere with intelligence.

ACCOMMODATION

People who have had polio are cautioned not to overexert weakened muscles. Therefore, they should not be expected to carry heavy loads or to perform tasks that require strength.

Ambulatory aids often slow the walking process, so allow time for slow progress. When walking beside a person who uses canes or crutches, stand far enough to the side to allow for "swing" in the devices. If the person uses a wheelchair, standard modification for wheelchair access will be necessary.

RESOURCES

Gazette International Networking Institute
4502 Maryland Avenue
St. Louis, MO 63108
(314) 361-0475

National Easter Seal Society
2023 West Ogden Avenue
Chicago, IL 60612

March of Dimes
1275 Mamaroneck Avenue
White Plains, NY 10605

PRADER–WILLI SYNDROME

Classification: Birth Defect

Prader–Willi syndrome occurs in one out of every five thousand births and is among the most common syndromes seen in birth defect clinics. The behavioral and physical manifestations of the syndrome indicate that it is a central nervous system disorder. As a result, behavior and learning potential are altered. Its cause has not been discovered, and at present there is no cure.

There appear to be two distinct stages in Prader–Willi syndrome. The first stage begins at birth and ends sometime between two and four years old. Stage one includes low birth weight; lack of muscle tone, size, and strength; mild deformities; and delayed motor development. Infants with this condition often appear completely unresponsive to their own environment and needs; they usually will not cry when hungry or even when in pain. Muscle strength seems to improve gradually. The ability to hold the head erect occurs late in the first year, sitting occurs around eleven months, and the ability to walk occurs at about two years. Speech is slow to develop. Most children begin talking in short sentences at about three and a half years.

Stage two begins with radical physical and behavioral changes between the ages of two and four. At this point the most pertinent characteristic of Prader–Willi syndrome surfaces: an insatiable appetite and total preoccupation with food. Foraging and food stealing are pervasive problems for most people with this condition.

The desire to eat is believed to be a dysfunction of the central nervous system. Although gorging is common, it is never followed by indigestion. To compound the problem, people with Prader–Willi syndrome require fewer calories to gain weight than do normal people. Poor muscle development usually prevents them from exercising properly. The child is usually obese before age five.

At approximately the same time as insatiable appetite occurs, a change in personality also takes place. The happy and affectionate child begins to be stubborn and have severe tantrums. In late adolescence, the child becomes violent and difficult to manage. Changes in routine cause immediate stress and behavior problems. In 90 percent of cases, there is some degree of mental retardation.

TREATMENT

There is no cure for Prader–Willi syndrome; however, its effects on the person can be modified with therapy, special education programs, diet management, and residential care.

EFFECT ON LIFESTYLE

If the extreme obesity that results from the insatiable appetite and obsession with food is not controlled, diabetes and heart problems may occur and these can result in a markedly shortened life span.

Because of obsession with obtaining food and potential behavior problems surrounding food, people with this condition have difficulty holding jobs. However, when placed in controlled, sheltered employment, they can be diligent workers. A person with Prader–Willi syndrome must remain in a lifelong restricted or closely supervised environment.

APPEARANCE

People with Prader–Willi syndrome have predictable physical characteristics including narrow forehead, almond-shaped eyes, triangular mouth, short stature, small tapering hands and feet that may be puffy in appearance, nearsightedness, and wandering eye.

Though they lack good muscle strength and coordination, few require the use of walkers or wheelchairs. The exception to this is the person who has developed severe spinal curvature due to uncontrolled weight and weak bones.

ACCOMMODATION

Persons with Prader–Willi syndrome will need a controlled environment, routine tasks, and employment appropriate to their mental ability.

RESOURCE

Prader–Willi Syndrome Association
5515 Malibu Drive
Edina, MN 55436
(612) 933-0113

SHORT STATURE

Classification: Birth Defect

Over one hundred different syndromes are characterized by short stature. Most relate in some way to the growth hormone secreted by the pituitary gland, which is controlled by that part of the brain called the hypothalamus.

The term preferred by people with retarded growth is "little people." Physicians have various terms to describe different conditions that result in short stature.

Dwarfs are defined as having an adult height of four feet ten inches or less. Achondroplastic dwarfs occur in one out of every ten thousand births. There is no sexual or racial predominance. A person with achondroplasia has a relatively normal torso and short arms and legs. The upper arms and thighs are more shortened then the forearms and lower legs. In addition, the head is large, the forehead is prominent, and the nose is flat at the bridge.

Werner syndrome is a disorder that causes premature aging. Affected people often die as early as thirty years old, but the average age at death is forty-seven. Many symptoms of this illness occur before the condition is diagnosed, including cessation of growth at about thirteen years of age. People with Werner's develop premature hardening of the arteries, osteoporosis, diabetes, and cataracts.

Weismann–Netter syndrome is a genetic disorder characterized by bowing of the legs, delayed ability to walk, and short stature. The symptoms of this condition often develop in childhood, but it is usually not diagnosed until the mid-teens.

Cretinism is a condition caused by iodine deficiency that results in impaired development of bones and impaired mental abilities.

TREATMENT

There is no specific treatment for short stature at this time. Injection of growth hormones does not increase height substantially. It is possible, however, to treat some of the problems associated with the various conditions.

EFFECT ON LIFESTYLE

There are definite difficulties in adjusting to a world geared to normal-sized people—everything is too big: clothing, furniture, shelves in the grocery store, automobiles. Door knobs and light switches often require tip-toes or a stool. In addition adult little people are often treated as if they were children. Because of unusual body structure, pregnant women often have to deliver their children by cesarean section.

ACCOMMODATION

The work area may have to be lowered to meet the needs of a little person. It isn't reasonable to expect people to climb up and down all day just to do their job. If the work is stationary, a platform may solve the problem. In other areas, make sure a safe step stool is handy, so the person isn't forced to climb on chairs or boxes to reach things. A stick can be used to push buttons that cannot be lowered. Most of all, remember that the person is an adult who is small.

RESOURCES

Little People of America
P.O. Box 633
San Bruno, CA 94066
(415) 589-0695

Human Growth Foundation
4720 Montgomery Lane, Suite 909
Bethesda, MD 20814
(301) 656-7540

SPINA BIFIDA

Classification: Birth Defect

Spina bifida (meaning "split spine") is one of the most common birth defects seen today. It occurs in one or two of every one thousand babies born in the United States. Babies with this defect are born more frequently in the eastern and southern states than in the western states. Great Britain and Ireland have a rate of four out of one thousand births. With the advances that have been made in our treatment methods in recent years, 80 to 95 percent of babies born with this condition now survive and grow into mature, productive members of society.

Spina bifida develops during the first four weeks after conception—often before a woman even knows she is pregnant. The condition is caused by a defect of the embryonic structure that will evolve into the brain and spinal cord. As the normal fetus grows, the edges of this structure (called the neural plate) begin to curl toward each other, forming a tube. As soon as this tube has developed into the spinal cord, bone and muscle begin to form around it as a protective barrier. In some fetuses, a small part of the neural plate does not form a tube and the bone cannot develop around it. The arches of the vertebrae that surround the spinal cord fail to develop. The spinal cord itself may be displaced outside the spinal canal. Nerves in this area are incompletely developed or damaged, and all nerves below the defect are usually affected. This nerve damage can result in varying degrees of paralysis, loss of skin sensation, bladder and bowel problems, and spine and limb deformities.

As many as 90 percent of the babies born with spina bifida also have, or soon develop, a condition called hydrocephalus. In this condition, spinal fluid accumulates in the brain because of a blockage that prevents it from draining out of the brain and spinal cord. If unrelieved, this fluid will put great pressure on the brain and will cause the skull to expand.

During the first days of the baby's life, surgeons will implant a shunt. The shunt will drain excess fluid from the baby's head into the abdominal area or a chamber in the heart, thus preventing brain damage and possibly death. New shunts will be implanted as the child grows and also in cases of malfunction or infection.

There are two main types of spina bifida: spina bifida occulta (hidden) and spina bifida manifesta (obvious).

Spina bifida occulta is somewhat rare and is the mildest form of the condition, with symptoms that range from none at all to mild bowel, bladder, or motor problems.

Spina bifida manifesta has two forms. In the relatively rare and milder form, the spinal cord is normal but the membranes that surround it bulge through the vertebrae into a sac visible on the baby's back. If nerves also bulge into this sac, minor muscle paralysis or bowel and bladder problems may be present.

In the most common and severe form of spina bifida manifesta, a portion of the undeveloped spinal cord itself protrudes through the back to form a sac. In some babies the sac is covered with skin; in others the tissue and nerves are exposed. This opening will be surgically closed, generally within the first twenty-four to forty-eight hours of life.

The nerve damage caused by this defect occurs while the spinal cord is developing and as the sac grows. The nerves may simply not develop properly or may be destroyed by pressure from the growing sac. The abnormal cord is unable to carry messages to and from the brain along existing nerves.

The spinal nerves that are affected by spina bifida extend out of the spinal cord at intervals all along its length. In a normal baby, these nerves send messages to the brain from the sense organs and from the brain to the muscles. In this way the body is able to feel temperature and pain and flex its muscles.

The nerves most commonly affected in spina bifida are the lumbar nerves, which activate motion and sense in the hip area, front of the legs, and tops of the feet.

TREATMENT

No treatment is needed in cases where the defect is slight. If there is an obvious lump but no paralysis or loss of feeling, it is possible for doctors to operate and prevent further damage. When a baby is born with severe spina bifida, doctors will remove the large, runny cyst and cover the wound with muscle and skin. The leg paralysis and lack of feeling associated with this condition can't be cured.

Soon after surgery, a physical therapist will teach the parents how to exercise the baby's legs to prepare it for walking with leg braces or crutches. Some children will need to use a wheelchair throughout life.

EFFECT ON LIFESTYLE

Kidney deterioration and chronic bladder infections are the greatest potential danger for children and adults with spina bifida.

Kidneys filter waste from the blood to form urine, and they return salts and other substances to the blood. The bladder stores this urine build-up. This part of the process is automatic. The sphincter muscle controls the opening of the bladder. When a normal person feels a full bladder, a signal is sent to the sphincter to relax, and the bladder contracts to release urine.

People with spina bifida are usually unable to control this process. Damaged nerves prevent them from feeling when the bladder is full. Some cannot relax their sphincters to let the urine out, while others have a sphincter that is always open so that urine leaks out.

Urine that accumulates in the bladder can back up into the kidneys, causing pressure that leads to life-threatening kidney deterioration. The retained urine is also a source of bacterial infection that attacks the kidneys.

People who have a nonrelaxing sphincter will generally use a process known as clean intermittent catheterization (CIC). In CIC a clean (not sterile) tube is inserted into the urethra to drain the urine from the bladder. This procedure is done every three to four hours, thereby keeping the bladder empty. In cases where CIC is not appropriate, surgeons can implant an artificial sphincter. The person presses through the skin to squeeze an implanted pump that releases the urine.

People with spina bifida also have some difficulty controlling bowel function. They are not able to sense when the bowel is full due to the loss of feeling. Because the anal muscle may be weak, the stool can move from within the bowel to the outside, without the person's awareness. Bowel function can be managed by adhering to special diets, taking medication, and establishing specific times for elimination. Accidents, however, can happen.

The lack of sensation characteristic of spina bifida creates the risk of infection from cuts and burns that are not felt and, therefore, not treated. Another major problem associated with loss of feeling is pressure sores. These sores occur when continuous heavy pressure is placed on a single area, reducing blood to the area and causing the skin to erode and die. This can be caused by sitting without moving for a long period or by shoes or braces that don't fit properly. Untreated sores can turn into ulcers that may require surgery.

People with spina bifida have normal hormone levels and sex drives. They are capable of having an orgasm. Women are able to have children, although they may find mobility more difficult during the last trimester. A woman with spina bifida has an increased chance of having a child with the same condition. Some 60 percent of males can function sexually and are fertile. The remaining 40 percent have a variety of problems, some of which can be surgically corrected.

Approximately 70 percent of spina bifida patients have normal intelligence. The other 30 percent are slightly to severely retarded.

APPEARANCE

Freedom of movement for people with spina bifida depends on many things, including the level of the defect, the extent of deformities, body build, age, weight, and desire to move. Some people will use wheelchairs and others walkers or braces.

Spina bifida can cause scoliosis, a sideways bending of the spine in some people. Others exhibit kyphosis, a forward bending of the spine that gives a hunchback look. These positions can range from hardly noticeable to definite, depending on whether surgery has been done to correct the problem.

Foot deformities (club foot, for example) and dislocated hips are common in people born with spina bifida. Weak muscles do not grow as fast as normal muscles, and this imbalance becomes more pronounced as the child grows. The strong muscles pull the joint out of place, and a deformity results.

Otherwise, expect normal appearance. If there is a facial or upper body deformity, problems in addition to spina bifida are present.

ACCOMMODATION

In general, useful walking is related to the level of paralysis. If the defect is above the 12th thoracic level, no practical walking is possible; therefore, a wheelchair will be the only mode of transport. From the 12th thoracic to the 4th lumbar area the defect will permit partial household or office walking with crutches and braces. Defects from the 4th lumbar to the 2nd sacral level will allow community ambulation (see Table 1).

Those people who use wheelchairs exclusively will need to change position frequently to prevent skin problems that result from unrelieved pressure. Expect a lot of shifting around in the chair.

For many people, especially young children, frequent emptying of the bladder is necessary. This will require a somewhat longer time in the restroom than you would expect in a nonaffected individual. Use of a catheter can be the cause of frequent kidney infections. Expect this illness to occur, but remember that kidney infections are not contagious.

Some people have problems with fine motor skills; they may not be able to write quickly or correctly. Try to separate thinking ability from the mechanical task of writing.

Table 1
Effects of Spina Bifida on Ambulation

SPINAL CORD SEGMENT	CONTROL LOST BELOW	RESULT	YOUNG CHILD	ADULT
12TH Thoracic	Trunk	Totally paralyzed lower limbs	Wheel chair	Wheelchair, No ambulation
1st & 2nd Lumbar	Pelvis	Hip flexor muscles affected	Crutches, Braces, Wheelchair	Wheelchair, Nonfunctional ambulation
3rd & 4th Lumbar	Hip	Quadriceps muscles affected	Crutches, Household ambulation, Wheelchair	50% Wheelchair, Household ambulation with crutches
5th Lumbar	Knee	Medial hamstring, Anterior tibial muscles affected	Crutches, Braces, Community Ambulation	Community Ambulation with crutches
1st Sacral	Foot	Lateral hamstrings	Community Ambulation	Community Ambulation
2nd & 3rd Sacral	Foot	Mild loss of intrinsic foot muscles	Normal	Community Ambulation, possible foot deformities

RESOURCES

Spina Bifida Association of America
343 South Dearborn, Suite 310
Chicago, IL 60604
(312) 663-1562

National Easter Seal Society, Inc.
2023 West Ogden Avenue
Chicago, IL 60612
(312) 243-8400

March of Dimes Birth Defects Foundation
1275 Mamaroneck Avenue
White Plains, NY 10605
(914) 428-7100

SPINAL CORD INJURIES
(Paraplegia—Quadriplegia)

Classification: Injury

The spinal cord in humans has a great deal of protection. Both the cord and the brain from which it comes lie deep within the body, protected by tough membranes, cushioned by shock-absorbing fluid, and surrounded by the bones of the skull and backbone. This defensive barrier is enough to protect the cord from the minor bumps and bruises of everyday life. Yet each year ten thousand pepole find the barrier will not protect them from severe bumps and falls. Approximately two hundred thousand Americans use wheelchairs because of an injury to the spinal cord. Spinal cord injuries usually happen to the young; an estimated two-thirds of those who are injured are thirty years old or younger. The majority are men.

The spine is actually a column of bones called vertebrae. This column is divided into groups: the top seven vertebrae are called the cervical vertebrae; the next twelve are the thoracic vertebrae; then come the five lumbar vertebrae; the five sacral vertebrae are fused together into one mass; finally, the four coccygeal vertebrae (often called the tail bone) are also fused. The cervical, thoracic, and lumbar vertebrae all have pads, called disks, between them that function as shock absorbers and facilitate bending and turning of the column.

The spinal cord, which is made up of thousands of tiny nerve fibers and is about the size of a man's little finger, runs through the vertebral column from the brain to the second lumbar vertebra. Nerves leaving the cord below this point form what is called the cauda equina (the horse's tail) (see Figures 6 and 7).

The peripheral nerves carry messages to and from the brain via the spinal cord. These nerves emerge from the cord via spaces between the vertebrae. Thus, injury to the vertebrae damages the nerves. Unfortunately, nerve cells (called neurons) in the brain and spinal cord are extremely sensitive. Unlike other cells in the body, injured nerves in the brain and spinal cord rarely recover from severe injury. They either die without being replaced or they do not recover sufficiently to resume normal operations. The result is that the human spinal cord does not heal itself.

Figure 6
Spine and Spinal Nerves, Posterior View

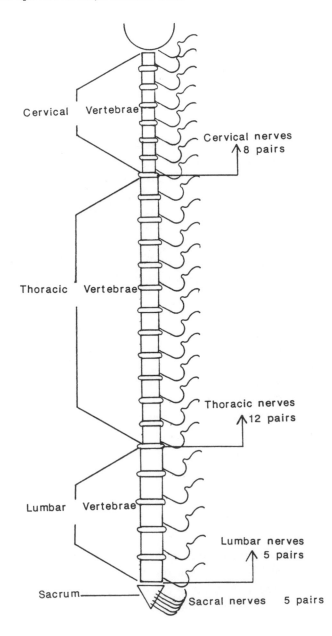

Cervical   Vertebrae

Cervical nerves
8 pairs

Thoracic   Vertebrae

Thoracic nerves
12 pairs

Lumbar   Vertebrae

Lumbar nerves
5 pairs

Sacrum

Sacral nerves   5 pairs

Figure 7
Single Vertebra

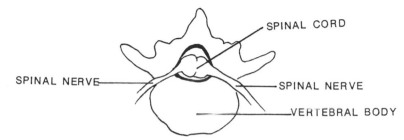

There are three common ways of damaging the spinal cord: flexion injury, hyperextension injury, and axial loading. In a flexion injury the head and neck are forced forward. As the vertebrae move, they rupture the spinal disk, which damages the cord. In a hyperextension injury, the head and neck are forced backward and the vertebrae themselves damage the cord. In axial loading, the force is on the top of the head, crushing the vertebrae together.

Usually the spinal cord is not severed in an accident; it is only bruised or crushed. In the first few hours after injury, however, the cord begins to destroy itself. First the cord swells. Then blood pressure in the damaged area drops sharply, reducing the supply of blood to the injured cells. Next, the center of the cord begins to hemorrhage; this hemorrhaging spreads outward, causing nerve cells to die. These dead nerves produce a gap in the cord. When scar tissue forms on both sides of the gap, the brain cannot send or receive signals beyond that point. The result is paralysis and/or the loss of sensation below the break. It can take two or three days for these events to occur. Therefore, the true extent of the injury is not known for several days after the accident.

The level of injury looks like the ragged edge of a broken cracker, and no two injuries have precisely the same "ragged edge." Therefore, function may be lost at point x but sensation may continue to point y because they are controlled by different nerves that were injured at different levels. This "ragged edge" is also why people who were injured at the same level on the spine have different capabilities. No two crackers break exactly the same way.

TREATMENT

Treatment for a spinal cord injury usually begins with stabilizing the vital life functions like heart rate, blood pressure, and breathing. When these things are under control, surgery will be done to reduce the damage to the cord.

If the injury is in the cervical area, a device called a "halo" will be attached to the skull in order to hold the neck immobile while the vertebrae heal. The top of the halo is screwed into the skull. Four rods extend downward from the halo into a padded support that rests on the shoulders and around the chest. This contraption can be somewhat disconcerting when seen for the first time.

Rehabilitation will start quite soon after surgery and will continue for many months. Some drug treatment will be offered to relieve the pain and reduce the muscle spasms associated with a spinal cord injury.

EFFECT ON LIFESTYLE

An injured spinal cord generally results in either quadriplegia or paraplegia. Quadriplegia means that the injury was at the cervical level and involves muscles in the upper and lower body. It can range from total paralysis to the inability to walk and a weak hand grip. Paraplegia means the injury was below the cervical level and involves muscles of the lower body only.

People who have had an injury to the spinal cord (usually called a "lesion") refer to the level of injury when describing their condition (C6 quadriplegic, cervical level 6, or T5 paraplegic, thoracic level 5). When a person uses two levels (i.e., C6/7), it indicates that one side of the body is less affected than the other.

Generally speaking, people injured at C1 to C4 will require mechanical help to breathe and will have no movement or sensation in the trunk or limbs; people injured at C5 to C8 will have some function in the arms and/or hands and no movement or sensation in the trunk or legs; people injured at T1 to T7 have involvement of the chest muscles and no movement or sensation below the chest; injuries at T8 to T12 involve the abdominal muscles and lower body; injuries at L1 to L5 involve the legs and hip area; injuries to S1 and below affect the bowel and bladder.

It is important to remember that function is lost or impaired at *and* below the level of injury. Most spinal cord injuries affect the bladder, bowels, and sexual organs. This is because the nerves that supply these functions come from the lower end of the spinal cord.

A "complete" injury implies that the damage was severe enough that the loss of both function and feeling is total. An "incomplete" injury implies that the damage was not as severe and the person has lost partial function and sensation from the point of injury down.

Pain can be an ongoing result of some injuries. A certain number of people with spinal cord injuries live with constant pain. Others may experience pain at the area of injury, but only when pressure is applied.

People with injuries at the cervical level don't have normal control of their internal thermostat. This presents two problems: first, it keeps them from sweating when they are hot; second, they do not always produce enough heat to keep warm. Sweat is the body's built-in cooling system, and when it doesn't work a person can dangerously overheat. When the person gets too hot or cold, it can take a long time to get back to normal.

There are several ongoing medical issues that affect the lifestyle of someone with a spinal cord injury. Wounds (cuts, burns, etc.) take longer to heal in paralyzed areas due to poor circulation. Pressure sores, urinary tract infections, and autonomic dysreflexia can quickly become life-threatening.

Pressure sores are caused by bone pressing against skin for a long period of time, leading to break down or ulceration of tissue. These ulcers can eat away skin and muscle to bone level. The extent of destruction may not be entirely visible and may undermine the superficial skin layers until a dangerous amount of flesh is eaten away. A person with a spinal cord injury will not be aware of this problem until it triggers autonomic dysreflexia.

Autonomic dysreflexia is a medical emergency that occurs in persons injured at T6 and above. Its cause is unknown, but the mechanism is well understood. Basically, there is an irritation of some type below the level of injury that sends an impulse to the spinal cord. The signal moves up the cord until blocked by the lesion. The nervous system wants to report the problem so the brain can call for action to fix it. The message can't get through and instead sets off a reflex action in the sympathetic nervous system. The nervous system becomes confused and out of balance, and the blood pressure soars.

The symptoms of autonomic dysreflexia are a pounding headache, profuse sweating above injury level, goose bumps, pupil contraction, nasal congestion, skin blotching, and a slow pulse. When these symptoms are present there is a potentially life-threatening situation developing, and the cause must be identified and corrected immediately.

Urinary tract infections are very common, especially when the bladder is not emptied completely during catheterization.

Sexual relations between partners are possible but may have to be somewhat creative so that both partners have their needs met. A spinal cord injury does not mean that a person has no need for a loving relationship. Many men who have a spinal cord injury can still father children, and women can become mothers.

APPEARANCE

Leg spasms are very common and do not indicate danger or voluntary movement. In fact, spasms can help keep the muscles toned and can be used in dressing or transferring out of the wheelchair.

Able-bodied people shift position slightly, even while sitting or sleeping, much more than they realize. This is done in response to the body's signal that there has been pressure on an area long enough and circulation needs to be improved. Paraplegics and low-level quadriplegics will tend to fidget in their chairs a great deal. This is not due to boredom but is a learned technique to relieve pressure and increase circulation. Using their arms or a mechanical aid, they will lift from the chair frequently and perhaps change the position of their legs.

If balance is a problem, the person may be strapped into the chair to keep from falling forward. It is common to see a person in a wheelchair slouching to one side or the other, or even strapped into an upright position. Many people will choose to strap their legs to the chair to prevent their feet from slipping off the foot rest and dragging on the ground.

If the injury affects the abdominal muscles, the person will have a pot-bellied look.

Dressing is sometimes very difficult for people who have high level injuries. Therefore, they tend to prefer clothing that is easy to put on rather than that which is the height of fashion.

An injury to the spinal cord does not affect intelligence. The person will have the same mental ability after injury as before no matter how high on the spine the injury occurs.

ACCOMMODATION

The individual is basically the same person after the trauma as before. Every personality is unique, and people should be treated for who they are, not for their disability. However, some individuals are injured in accidents where there may be other issues to deal with in addition to their paralysis. Issues such as the possible death of others in the accident, law suits, and family problems are common. People are not always aware of all the dynamics a person is experiencing and should respect the coping mechanisms the person uses to deal with them.

People who have high-level injuries may still be able to write and feed themselves, but they will use the muscles of the upper arm or shoulder for motion. If this is the case, allow plenty of space for the arm swing that is necessary.

Plans need to be made to assist someone who uses a wheelchair in the event fire or natural disaster prohibits using an elevator. If you are in an area of the country where it gets very hot, provide a fan for use in case the air conditioning system goes down. Structural accommodations will need to be made for the wheelchair.

RESOURCES

National Spinal Cord Injury Foundation
369 Elliot Street
Newton Upper Falls, MA 02164

Paralyzed Veterans of America
4330 East-West Highway, Suite 300
Washington, DC 20014

International Medical Society of Paraplegia
E and S Livingstone
43-45 Annandale Street
Edinburgh EH7 4AT
Scotland

STROKE
(Cerebrovascular Accident)

Classification: Injury

A stroke is an injury to the nervous system that occurs when the brain does not receive an adequate supply of oxygen and nutrients in a specific area. Strokes are the third leading cause of death in industrialized nations. Each year, approximately five hundred thousand people in the United States have a stroke. About 2.5 million have survived a stroke and lead relatively active lives.

Most strokes are caused by blood clots that slow the flow of blood in the brain and cause irreversible injury to brain cells. The most common type of stroke is caused by a blood clot that forms in one of the arteries of the brain itself. In some cases, however, a blood clot forms in the heart or in some other blood vessel and travels to the brain. The result in either case is that blood cannot flow around the clot in sufficient quantity to provide nourishment to the cells downstream.

In a relatively small number of cases, a stroke results from a hemorrhage within the brain due to a blood vessel that ruptures from injury or anatomical weakness. This condition is referred to as a cerebral hemorrhage.

Regardless of the cause, the effects of a stroke are the result of reduced blood flow to the nerve cells of the brain. Brain cells require a constant flow of oxygen and nutrient-rich blood, and any decrease in this flow will produce irreversible damage.

The actual damage caused by a stroke is dependent on two factors: the site of the problem and the amount of brain tissue involved. Unfortunately, brain cells do not regenerate. Nevertheless, in some cases, losses can be recovered by retraining the cells that have not been damaged or possibly by activating new or unused pathways within the brain.

Strokes caused by blood clots occur most often in the older population. Cerebral hemorrhage occurs in young people as well as older people. Unfortunately, cerebral hemorrhage is often far more serious than a stroke caused by blood clot. In fact, 40 percent die within the first month after hemorrhage.

When a stroke is caused by a blood clot, a series of events takes place. When the flow of blood diminishes, the membrane that surrounds each affected cell begins to leak potassium and an energy-producing chemical called ATP. This fluid collects in the spaces between the blood vessel and the cell. As the amount of fluid increases it becomes more and more difficult for oxygen and nutrients to get from the blood vessel to the cells. When the flow of life-giving oxygen and nutrients stops, the cell dies. The cells farther downstream from the clot may begin to seek nourishment from alternative vessels and may ultimately return to normal.

The effects caused by stroke due to hemorrhage are the result of abnormal pressure on the cells. Bleeding in the brain is like bleeding in any other area of the body. After a few minutes the blood forms a hard clot and active bleeding will stop. This clot, however, will put pressure on some cells, distort their normal shape, and prevent oxygen and nutrients from entering the cells upon which it presses.

TREATMENT

Rehabilitation can begin as soon as the person is medically stable. Initial efforts involve proper positioning and passive exercises to prevent additional disability. The goal of the initial therapy is to pave the way for the rehabilitation team.

A complete rehabilitation team may include a physical therapist, occupational therapist, speech-language specialist, psychiatrist, and social worker. This team will work with the brain's inherent ability to overcome injury.

Brain cells that are destroyed during a stroke cannot be repaired. However, neurological function that has been lost can return to a certain degree because the brain is adaptive in its structure and function. It can reform its ways of performing vital activities by forming new pathways and alternative connections that bypass the injured cells. This requires intensive retraining in a variety of areas in the brain and will not be accomplished overnight.

Virtually everyone who has had a stroke experiences debilitating emotions that interfere with recovery. The psychiatrist can provide guidance and support during this extended recovery effort.

EFFECT ON LIFESTYLE

The left and right halves of the brain look exactly alike but control very different functions of the body. Therefore, the location of the stroke, not the stroke itself, will determine the effect on lifestyle.

The left hemisphere of the brain controls the majority of functions on the right side of the body. A stroke in the left hemisphere can:

Cause a variety of language problems (difficulty speaking or understanding speech, writing, reading, and gestures)

Produce uncoordinated movement of the mouth, lips, tongue, and vocal cords that may make speech difficult

Result in a slow, cautious personality

Produce memory gaps for recent and/or past events

Result in loss of muscle function and coordination on the right side of the face, trunk, and limbs

Impair the sense of heat, cold, pain, and position on the right side

Create blind spots in the right visual field

The right side of the brain controls most of the functions of the left side of the body (see Figure 8). Injury to the right hemisphere can produce:

Impaired awareness of spatial relationships and a poor perception of distance

Impulsive behavior, quick movements, imprecise movement, and judgment errors

Weakness, paralysis, or lack of coordination of the face, trunk, and limbs on the left side of the body

Impaired sense of touch, pain, temperature, and position sense on the left side

Poor awareness of limb position in space

Figure 8
Right Side of the Brain

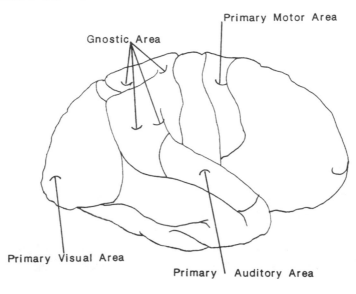

Denial of the presence of a part of the body
Difficulty dressing appropriately
Visual misperceptions, a loss of recognition of the left side of the visual field

A stroke in the front or interior of the brain may produce such symptoms as:

Severe paralysis of the leg and lesser paralysis of the arm on the side opposite
  the injury
Loss of feeling in the opposite toes, foot, and leg
Loss of control over bowel and/or bladder function
Balance problems
Loss of whispered speech, or loss of all communication ability
Lack of spontaneous emotions
Memory loss or impairment

A stroke in the rear portion of the brain may produce:

Visual disturbances
Impaired sensation of hot and cold

Impaired ability to read and/or name objects

Vertigo

Balance problems

Paralysis of the face or limbs

Strokes that affect the deep brain centers that control the heart, lungs, and other vital systems are called brainstem strokes and usually result in death.

APPEARANCE

Most people who have had a stroke will have weakness or paralysis on one side of the body. This can range from a foot that drags when the person walks to total loss of ambulation and use of a wheelchair. Often there is paralysis or drooping on one side of the face.

The most striking things about a person who is post-stroke usually revolve around communication; ability to relate to themselves, others, and the space around them; and personality changes.

Communication problems are many and varied, and it is important to remember that deficits in one area do not mean there will be deficits in other areas or that there is intellectual impairment. People may be able to use one word at a time or simple phrases but be unable to form sentences. They may be able to understand simple words but are confused by complex conversation. Some people will have no problem with speech but will be incapable of reading or using the phone for routine communication. Some people will lose the ability to make the sounds necessary for speech but understand all conversation entirely, while others have problems understanding the meaning of words.

People with impairment of spatial perception will sometimes attempt to move quickly and misjudge distance. Others will completely ignore the existence of one or more parts of their own body—not realizing what it is or that it is attached to them. If you are standing on the "bad" side of someone with spatial problems in vision, you are in an area that cannot be perceived and you will be ignored.

Some people will become very impulsive in their behavior after a stroke; others will become slow and cautious. These personality changes can be very difficult to understand—especially for post-stroke individuals. They may attempt activities that are not reasonable and then not understand what made them try it. On the other hand, people who were outgoing and are now timid and cautious may not understand the reason they are uncertain.

Mood swings are not uncommon for the person who has had a stroke but should, with patience and support, improve over time.

ACCOMMODATION

If language has been compromised, keep communication simple. Speak slowly and clearly, and avoid communicating in the presence of distractions. Be sure to position yourself so that your face and body can be seen. Be patient when words come slowly. Be encouraging. It will be helpful to review the chapters on speech and hearing disorders in this book.

A shoulder rest for the telephone receiver will permit the person with paralysis on one side to hold the phone and write at the same time. If writing is a problem, a cassette tape player will allow the person to send messages orally instead of in writing. The section on accommodation in the Introduction will provide further insight.

For those who use a walker, ramps will be necessary in place of stairs. Standard accommodation for wheelchairs will need to be made for those who use them.

RESOURCE

American Heart Association
7320 Greenville Avenue
Dallas, TX 75231

STUTTERING

Classification: Unknown

There are more than 15 million people in the world who stutter and, for reasons as yet unknown, boys are four times as likely to be affected as girls.

Stuttering is a condition in which the smooth flow of speech is interrupted by abnormal periods with no sound, repetitions, or prolongations of sounds or syllables. Researchers today attribute stuttering to problems in the control of the muscles of speech, not on psychological problems as had been thought in the past. The reasons for this control problem may be different in each case.

Stuttering usually begins after a child has developed the basics of speech and is beginning to be fluent, though occasionally stuttering arises in older children or even adults.

There are over one hundred muscles involved in the production of speech. Breathing muscles in the chest produce the pressure that drives air up the windpipe across the larynx, or voice box. At the larynx, air passes between two folds of tissue called vocal cords. The passing air causes the cords to vibrate, and the vibrating cords convert air flow into audible sound. The shape of the cords and the amount of tension on them determine the pitch of the voice (how high or low it sounds). Speech is further refined by the relative shape and position of the lips, tongue, jaws, cheeks, and palate.

The larynx has two opposing sets of muscles that normally work in a coordinated and reciprocal manner: one set contracts while the other set relaxes. When these two sets of muscles fight for control of the larynx (both sets contracting or relaxing at the same time) stuttering occurs. However, scientists are unclear on whether this fight between the muscles is the cause of the failure to speak fluently or is a reaction to the failure of speech.

All people who stutter can speak fluently some of the time. Most can also speak in unison with others, sing, and whisper smoothly. People who stutter can usually speak easily when they are prevented from hearing their own voice, when practicing alone in front of a mirror, or when talking to a pet. People who stutter have also been known to stop stuttering for no apparent reason.

Whatever the cause of the problem, people who stutter usually have their worst moments under stressful conditions, such as talking over the telephone, speaking in public or to strangers, or when they are under emotional strain.

TREATMENT

Stuttering is not a disease, therefore, the term "cure" is inappropriate. There are several approaches that can lead to improved fluency and success in communicating. Biofeedback techniques to help people who stutter learn to relax their throat muscles at will is one of the new treatment methods. Also enjoying some success are programs that emphasize modifying sound production at the larynx. People are taught to speak lower, softer, slower, and smoother. Some people have success when taught to slow their overall speech rate in a specific manner.

EFFECT ON LIFESTYLE

The effect of stuttering is more psychological than physical. People who stutter tend to avoid social situations and often have feelings of inferiority. The inability to speak fluently also tends to reduce employment opportunities in areas where the ability to communicate freely is critical such as police, fire, or emergency dispatchers, airline pilots, or jobs that require extensive use of the telephone.

APPEARANCE

There are no outward signs until stutterers begin to speak. Then their appearance is dramatic. As they struggle to get the words out, they may contort their whole face, the jaw may tremble repeatedly, the mouth is open, the tongue may protrude, and the eyes move rapidly from side to side. The tension can spread throughout the entire body as the overwhelming struggle to say a particular word occurs.

ACCOMMODATION

There are no mechanical or structural accommodations that will make life easier for people who stutter. Listen patiently and carefully to what is being said, and do not focus on how it is being said. Don't look away or hurry the speaker. Never fill in words for the person who stutters. Anything that creates pressure increases the problem.

RESOURCES

American Speech-Language-Hearing Association
10801 Rockville Pike
Rockville, MD 20852
(301) 897-5700

National Association for Hearing and Speech Action
6110 Executive Boulevard, Suite 1000
Rockville, MD 20852
(301) 897-8682

Speech Foundation of America
152 Lombardy Road
Memphis, TN 38111
(901) 452-7343

TOURETTE'S SYNDROME

Classification: Birth Defect

Tourette's syndrome is a neurological disorder characterized by involuntary movements, sounds, and inappropriate words, all generally referred to as "tics."

The cause of this condition has not been definitively established, but it is known to be inherited as a dominant gene that may produce different symptoms in different people. Current research indicates that the defective gene causes abnormal metabolism of at least one brain chemical called dopamine.

It is estimated that 100,000 Americans have Tourette's syndrome in a serious form and as many as one in two hundred people has a milder form. Males are affected three times as often as females.

There are two broad categories of tics: simple and complex. A simple tic is manifested as eye blinking, head jerking, facial grimacing, throat clearing, sniffing, tongue clicking, and the like. Complex tics usually begin as facial movements. As the condition progresses, there may be repeated stretching of the neck, stamping of feet, or twisting and bending. Eventually the person produces strange, uncontrollable, and unacceptable sounds, including shouted obscenities or constantly repeating the words of other people. Occasionally the person may touch other people excessively or exhibit obsessive-compulsive traits. A few people bang their heads against hard objects and exhibit other self-destructive behaviors. These are all involuntary actions.

Most people with Tourette's syndrome have the ability to delay expression of these tics for a few seconds up to a few hours. However, the tic must be expressed, and delays often cause more severe outbursts of symptoms. Some people have either a complete remission or at least a great improvement of their symptoms in their late teens or early twenties. A normal life span can be anticipated.

TREATMENT

Most people with Tourette's syndrome are not physically disabled by their tics or behavioral symptoms. Those who have symptoms that interfere with function can take medication to relieve symptoms. Psychotherapy can help a person with this condition to cope. Some behavior therapies teach the substitution of one tic with another that is more socially acceptable.

EFFECT ON LIFESTYLE

Early diagnosis and treatment are essential to avoid psychological harm. If the symptoms are viewed as bizarre, disruptive, or frightening, they provoke ridicule and rejection by peers, teachers, employers, and occasionally even parents.

APPEARANCE

The person with Tourette's syndrome will appear normal when not in the throes of a tic. When involved in a tic, the person will move one or more body parts excessively, produce strange and sometimes unacceptable sounds, and perhaps engage in self-destructive behavior. It must be remembered that the person is not in control of these actions.

ACCOMMODATION

People with Tourette's syndrome need a tolerant work and school environment that has minimum stress. Time limits are a source of stress that can be eliminated. The use of tape recorders and computers eliminates the need to write, which can be stressful for some people. Most of all, access to a private place when tics become overwhelming is very helpful.

RESOURCES

Tourette Syndrome Association, Inc.
41-02 Bell Boulevard,
Bayside, NY 11361
(212) 224-2999

National Institute of Neurological Disorders
Building 31, Room 8A16
National Institutes of Health
Bethesda, MD 20892
(301) 496-5751

VISION IMPAIRMENT

Classification: Illness or Injury

Nearly 30 million people in the world are blind. A similar number are visually handicapped. In the United States the number of people with severe visual impairment is around 3.5 million; of those, approximately

1.1 million are legally blind. Four-fifths of this vision loss is entirely preventable.

Vision depends on light. The light reflects from objects and enters the eye through a clear covering called the cornea, whose purpose is to focus the light onto the retina. The iris, the part of the eye that gives it its color, expands and contracts to control the amount of light that reaches the retina. The lens enables the eye to focus on objects that are varying distances from it and also fine-tunes the focus. The retina is the inside lining of the eye and functions much like the film in a camera. Near the center back of the eye, the most light-sensitive point of the retina, is the macula where the sharpest vision is achieved. This is the area that gives us central vision. The optic nerve receives all these visual sensations recorded on the retina and carries them to the brain where they are defined (see Figure 9).

Figure 9
Parts of the Eye

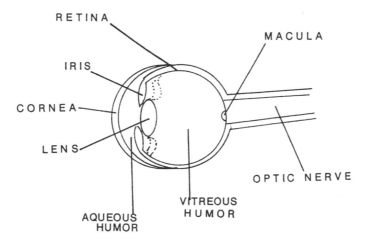

Central vision is what we use when we look straight at an object. It allows us to read and see what we are looking at. Peripheral vision allows us to see "out of the corner" of our eye. While reading this page you could still see a person enter the room with peripheral vision.

Legal blindness does not necessarily mean total blindness. A person is legally blind if central vision *in the better eye*, with optimal correction, is no better than 20/200 (they can just see the top "E" on an eye chart from 20 feet away) or if peripheral vision *in the better eye* with optimal correction, is no greater than 20 degrees in diameter. A person who is totally blind in one eye or has a missing eye is not legally blind unless the remaining eye meets one of those two criteria.

There are many causes of vision loss. Glaucoma, diabetic retinopathy, and macular degeneration are the three main causes of blindness in the United States. Retinal detachment, a fourth cause, will affect one out of every ten thousand people each year in the United States. The chief cause of bilateral blindness in the Third World is cataracts. Vitamin A deficiency accounts for 70 percent of the cases of childhood blindness worldwide. Loss of vision may also result from damage to the optic nerve caused by head trauma. In the majority of trauma cases, the loss of vision is immediate, remains stable, and is not treatable. Unless things change, the number of people who are blind will double by the year 2025.

Glaucoma

There are certain risk factors that may make some people more prone to developing glaucoma, including diabetes, hardening of the arteries, anemia, and family history of the condition. Black people are also at an increased risk of glaucoma for reasons as yet unknown.

When a person looks at an object, the image is carried to the brain by the optic nerve. The optic nerve is like a cable with a million wires in it; each wire carries a part of the picture to the brain where the parts are assembled into the picture. Glaucoma can produce damage to these "wires," causing blind spots to develop in areas of vision. People seldom notice these tiny blind areas until considerable damage has been done.

A clear water-like fluid called aqueous humor flows through the inner eye constantly. If the drainage part of this system gets blocked, the fluid pressure within the inner eye is increased and causes damage to the optic nerve. This increased pressure due to fluid buildup is known as glaucoma and is what damages the optic nerve. There are four ways this "drainpipe" can get blocked.

First, it can simply get smaller due to deposits or aging. This partial blockage causes a slow increase of pressure within the eye known as open-angle glaucoma. Chronic open-angle glaucoma can steal vision so slowly that the person is unaware of trouble until the optic nerve is seriously damaged.

Second, the outlet may have been abnormal since birth. A child's eye has more elasticity than an adult's eye, so when the pressure builds in the child's eye it simply enlarges. The front of the eye may look cloudy, the infant may be sensitive to light, and the eyes may tear a lot.

Third, the iris may press up against the drainage area and close if off. In this case, there is sudden, complete blockage of outflow, resulting in acute angle-closure glaucoma. Unless this condition is quickly corrected, blindness can result in a day or two. Fortunately, the symptoms of this condition are such that most people will realize that something is seriously wrong. Symptoms include blurred vision, severe pain, rainbow halos around light, nausea, and vomiting.

Fourth, other conditions including injury, certain drugs, tumors, hemorrhages in the eye, and inflammations can cause pressure to build up in the eye leading to glaucoma.

TREATMENT

Glaucoma is usually controlled by eye drops or by pills. However, to be effective, these medications must be taken faithfully and continuously. Treatment is used to prevent further damage from occurring and to preserve existing vision. Damage already caused by glaucoma cannot be reversed. If medication isn't working or is causing unexpected side effects, it is possible to treat glaucoma with surgery. In some cases, almost painless surgery can be done with a laser beam; in other cases, standard surgical procedures can be used to form a new drainage canal.

Diabetic Retinopathy

Diabetic retinopathy is the term used for all abnormalities of the retina caused by diabetes. One abnormality is the deterioration of the blood vessels nourishing the retina. Some vessels decrease in size, and others enlarge and form sacs that obstruct the flow of blood. These weakened blood vessels may leak fluid or blood. In some cases this leaking fluid collects in the macula and results in legal blindness.

Another abnormality is the result of new blood vessels growing on the surface of the retina or the optic nerve. These fragile little vessels may rupture and bleed into the vitreous, a clear gel-like substance that fills the center of the eye, thereby blocking the retina from the light and causing images to be distorted and blurred.

A third abnormality is the tendency of the macula to swell and thicken, decreasing its ability to provide clear central vision.

TREATMENT

Various treatments for diabetic retinopathy are possible. In some cases the physician will use laser surgery to seal or photocoagulate the leaking blood vessels. This treatment does not require an incision and is often performed in the doctor's office.

If laser treatment is not possible due to the large amount of blood leakage, a surgical procedure called a vitrectomy is possible. This approach involves removing the blood-filled gel and replacing it with a clear artificial solution.

Vision loss caused by diabetes depends on several factors: the length of time the person has had the disease, the kind of diabetes it is, and the quality of blood sugar level control. The physician will take all these things into consideration along with the amount of damage done to the retina before deciding on the proper treatment.

Macular Degeneration

Macular degeneration is damage or breakdown of the macula, the source of central vision. The eye still sees objects to the side because peripheral vision is not affected. For this reason macular degeneration does not result in total blindness but rather a "blind spot" in the central field of vision.

The most common form of this condition is called involutional macular degeneration and is usually associated with aging. The second most common form is called exudative macular degeneration and is asociated with formation of scar tissue due to ruptured blood vessels in the eye. Occasionally injury, infection, or inflammation may also damage the delicate tissue of the macula.

TREATMENT

There is no cure for involutional macular degeneration. However, laser surgery has been used to retard the spread of the exudative form, but only when caught in the very early stages of the condition.

Retinal Detachment

Most cases of retinal detachment are caused by small tears or holes in the retina. Normal aging can sometimes cause the retina to thin and deteriorate, but more often shrinkage of the vitreous substance is responsible for deterioration and retinal tears. The vitreous gel is attached to the retina in several places around the inside wall of the eye. As the gel shrinks, it may pull a piece of the retina away, leaving a tear or hole. Once a tear is present in the retina, watery fluid from the vitreous area may pass through the hole and lodge between the retina and the back wall of the eye. This causes the retina to detach from the back of the eye. Once detached, that area will not work properly, and there will be a blur or a blind spot in vision.

TREATMENT

If retinal detachment has not yet occurred, it may be prevented by prompt treatment. Tears can be sealed using laser photocoagulation or by freezing. Once the retina becomes detached, it must be surgically repaired. Such operations vary in nature depending on the extent of the detachment and damage. However, over 90 percent of all retinal detachments can be reattached successfully; the person thereby retains some degree of sight. The amount of vision that will finally return usually isn't known until approximately six months after surgery and will vary depending on how much detachment was present and how long the condition had existed.

EFFECT ON LIFESTYLE

The person who is blind and has acclimated well has very few practical restrictions on lifestyle. The real restriction is imposed by the way society treats a person who is blind. All other things being equal, there is no reason a person who is blind cannot be a fully ambulatory, self-supporting, contributing member of society.

Many people assume that all people who are blind can read braille. However, recent studies reveal that the number of people literate in braille is far fewer than expected. With the number of books available on audio tape, many people who are blind choose to read by listening.

ACCOMMODATION

Low-vision aids fall into two general categories: optical and adaptive. Optical aids magnify the objects being viewed. Adaptive aids modify objects or the environment for easier use by people with sight loss. With either of these two approaches, it is best to "try before you buy." What works for one person may not help another.

Technology for computer users with vision impairment is developing at a rapid pace. Programs exist that allow the computer to give and receive voice commands, magnify the screen from two to sixteen times, and read aloud areas of the screen display.

Interpersonal accommodation should follow these guidelines:

If a blind person appears to need assistance, identify yourself and offer help.

Give clear directions as to what they are to do or where they are to go. Don't avoid the words "look" and "see"; there are no reasonable substitutes.

When you're going to leave, tell the person you are leaving.

A guide dog is responsible for its master's safety; do not pet or otherwise distract the animal. Also remember that seeing eye dogs are allowed to go anywhere their owner goes.

To guide a blind person, let him or her take your elbow and follow the motion of your body. Walk about one-half step ahead and identify steps, curbs, or obstacles as you approach them. Pause briefly at steps or curbs.

Go up or down stairs one step ahead of the person being guided.

In areas too narrow for walking side by side, tell the person about the situation and direct him or her to get behind you by bending your arm backward so your hand is partly behind your back. If circumstances make this position impractical, have the person who is blind hold your shoulder.

When people who are blind are to enter a car, guide their hand to the leading object, door handle, or door edge, and they will do the rest.

When helping those who are blind to a chair, simply guide their hand to the chair arm or back.

Keep doors closed or wide open. A partially open door is among the most dangerous obstacles a person who is blind can encounter.

RESOURCES

American Foundation for the Blind
15 West 16th Street
New York, NY 10011
(800) 232-5463

Helen Keller International
Same as above

American Council of the Blind
(800) 424-8666

International Eye Foundation
7801 Norfolk Avenue
Bethesda, MD 20814

Operation Eyesight International
P.O. Box 123, Station M
Calgary, Alberta TIP 2H6
Canada

Royal Commonwealth Society for the Blind
Commonwealth House, Haywards, Heath
West Sussex RH16, 3AZ
England

WHO, Prevention of Blindness Programme
1211 Geneva 27
Switzerland

WERNICKE–KORSAKOFF SYNDROME

Classification: Illness

Wernicke–Korsakoff syndrome is a nonreversible and nontreatable illness affecting approximately 3 percent of the adult population of the United States. The rate of occurrence in other countries in which alcohol is consumed is comparable. In countries in which famine or inadequate nutrition is a problem, the rate is considerably higher.

Wernicke–Korsakoff syndrome—which can profoundly affect mental and physical ability and can also be fatal—is the result of a nutritional deficiency of thiamine (vitamin B1) and usually occurs in alcoholics. The condition is actually two distinct diseases: Wernicke disease and Korsakoff psychosis.

Wernicke disease is a neurological disorder that begins very abruptly. Its symptoms, which may occur separately or together, include involuntary horizontal movement of the eyes; vision problems such as double vision; unsteadiness while standing or walking; extreme fatigue; confusion; and absence of emotion.

Korsakoff psychosis is characterized by problems with learning, memory, and behavior changes.

The condition often develops when alcohol displaces food in the diet, thereby eliminating the source of thiamine. Alcohol also adds its own carbohydrate calories, increasing the body's need for thiamine.

The normal adult body on a thiamine-free diet depletes its reserves of thiamine in about eighteen days. Left untreated, Wernicke disease patients often progress to a coma and die.

TREATMENT

The condition is not reversible and not treatable. Caught before the disease takes hold, the condition may be prevented with infusions of large amounts of vitamin B1.

EFFECT ON LIFESTYLE

Without thiamine, chemical reactions in the body begin to fail. Nerve impulses are not transmitted, and blood flow in the brain is reduced. Wernicke–Korsakoff syndrome is usually hopeless after it strikes.

ACCOMMODATION

If the process that leads to Wernicke–Korsakoff syndrome is stopped before the disease takes hold, the person may have the residual effects of alcoholism or starvation, and accommodation may require adjustments for loss of body strength, reduced mental quickness, and some memory loss. Once the disease has taken hold, the person most likely will withdraw from society and eventually die.

RESOURCES

At this time there are no special support groups for people with Wernicke–Korsakoff syndrome or their families.

Appendix A: Common Medications

This appendix lists the medications commonly used to control specific conditions. Wherever possible, the generic and sales names are given. The medications listed here are generally available by prescription only.

FOR CONTROL OF SEIZURES

Diphenylhydation (Dilantin) for grand mal
Ethosuximide (Zaronthin) for petit mal
Paramethadione (Paradione) for petit mal
Phenobarbital (Luminal or stental) for grand mal
Primidone (Mysoline) for grand mal

FOR MANAGING ASTHMA

Epinephrine, ephedrine, isoproterenol, terbutaline, albuterol, metaproterenol (all are B2-adrenergic agents)
Theophylline and its derivatives
Bronchodilator inhalers like Ventolin, Vanceril, Alupent
Prednisone and other corticosteroids
Cromolyn sodium

ANTI-INFLAMMATORY MEDICINES

ACTH (corticotrophin) injection only
Cortisone

Dexamethasone
Hydrocortisone
Prednisone
Trimcinolone

FOR MANAGING ANXIETY

Barbiturates like phenobarbital
Chlorodiazepoxide hydrochloride (Librium, Valium)
Hydroxyzine (Vistaril)
Meprobamates (Miltown, Equanil)

FOR MANAGING DEPRESSION (three kinds)

Tricyclic antidepressants
   Amitriptyline (Elavil, Endep)
   Desipramine (Pertofrane, Norpramin)
   Doxepin (Sinequan, Adapin)
   Imipramine (Tofranil, Imanate, Presamine)
   Nortriptyline (Aventyl)
   Protriptyline (Vivactil)
Monoamine oxidase (MAO) inhibitors
   Isocarboxazid (Marplan)
   Phenelzine (Nardil)
   Tranylcypromine (Parnate)
Lithium

FOR HYPERACTIVITY

Dextroamphetamine (Dexedrine)
Methylphenidate hydrochloride (Ritalin)
Pemoline (Cylert)

MISCELLANEOUS

Insulin for diabetes
Diuretics for prevention or elimination of swelling
Amphetamines for appetite suppression
Antitumor drugs for cancer

NOTE: Many medications have a variety of uses. Therefore, use of one of the substances listed here is not conclusive evidence of a specific condition.

Appendix B: Overview of the Americans with Disabilities Act

The Americans with Disabilities Act of 1990 was written to bring people who have one or more disabilities into the mainstream of American life. That means a great deal more than just getting a job. It also means the opportunity to use public transportation, communicate freely, participate in retail consumerism, and enjoy cultural and recreational opportunities.

In order to make this lifestyle a reality, the government has asked a few things of this country's employers, retailers, and others who interact with the public:

1. *Equal Opportunity.* The right of a person with a disability to be treated the same as a person without a disability, insofar as that is possible.

2. *Reasonable Accommodation.* The help an employer must provide to people who would be unable to compete in the job market without it. Think of this as being the same as a handicap in golf. It simply is a means of allowing all players to compete on an equal basis.

3. *Reasonable Access.* The modifications a public accommodation must make in order that a person with a disability may enjoy access to the goods or services of that establishment.

The equal opportunity requirement is absolute, but not really new. The Civil Rights Act of 1964 stipulates equal opportunity for everyone regardless of sex, race, color, national origin, or religion. The ADA simply adds disability to the list. Reasonable access and reasonable accommodation are new, however, and are different in every situation.

The primary difference between access and accommodation is that access has specific requirements that must meet the letter of the law—generally in terms of architecture. Accommodation usually is on an individual basis; therefore, the law is intentionally very general and open.

A lot has been written about job accommodations for "qualified individuals with a disability." That phrase prompts two important questions: What is a disability? What does "qualified" mean?

The definition of a disability under the ADA is: a person with a physical or mental impairment that substantially limits one or more of the major life activities of that person, or a record of having this impairment, or being regarded as having such an impairment. Now let's define the definition.

A "physical or mental impairment" is any physiological disorder or condition, anatomical loss, or cosmetic disfigurement that affects one or more of the body's systems (musculoskeletal system, respiratory system [including organs of speech], neurological system, cardiovascular system, digestive system, reproductive system, genitourinary system, blood or lymphatic systems, endocrine system, skin) or any mental or psychological disorder, such as mental retardation, emotional illness, mental illness, organic brain syndrome, learning disability, drug addiction (to a limited extent), or alcoholism (to a limited extent).

A person is considered to have a disability even if medications or assistive devices completely control the condition. For instance, if people have diabetes but take medication that keeps it completely under control, they still are covered under the law. If people have a hearing impairment but use a hearing aid that enables them to hear clearly, they still are protected under the ADA.

The ADA does list some conditions that are specifically *not* considered disabilities, including transvestism, transsexualism, pedophilia, exhibitionism, voyeurism, gender identity disorders, compulsive gambling, kleptomania, pyromania, disorders resulting from the current use of illegal drugs, and active abuse of alcohol. Persons with short-term illnesses such as measles, influenza, or even pheumonia are not covered even if they have a characteristic predisposition to the illness. An injury such as a broken bone that is reasonably expected to heal is also not covered.

The root cause of some conditions must be identified in order to classify them. For instance, if people cannot read because of a learning disability, they are protected under the ADA; but if they cannot read because they didn't go to school, they are not protected. A broken bone is not a disability in and of itself, but if it is the result of osteogenesis imperfecta then it is a covered condition.

A "substantial limitation of major life activities" refers to such things as caring for oneself, walking, seeing, hearing, doing manual tasks, breathing, learning, and working. The key word, however, is "substantial" and means a significant restriction when compared with an average person. A person who is winded after running a mile doesn't have a disability because he can't run two miles. Most of us can't. But a person who is winded after walking across the room is disabled, because most of us can do that. Remember, this judgment cannot be made on the basis of any medical intervention. Even if people with a prosthesis can walk as well as anyone else, they have a disability because they have lost a limb.

The duration of a condition must also be taken into account when determining substantial limitation. An acute case of bronchitis may result in a person being winded after walking across a room, but the bronchitis can be completely cured in a relatively short time and is not, therefore, a "substantial limitation."

Work is considered to be a major life activity, but the inability to do a specific job is not a disability if the person is not substantially limited in any other major life activity. If a professional tennis player can no longer play tennis due to a bad case of "tennis elbow," that person is not considered disabled because he is unable to work in the narrow range of jobs that require swinging a racquet. A carpenter who develops a fear of heights (acrophobia) and can no longer work on the second or third floors of a construction site is not considered disabled because that person can still perform a number of jobs in one-story buildings and is not disabled in any other way. A person who is too obese to qualify as a flight attendant is not disabled because that person can perform other work and is not substantially limited in any other way.

A person with a *record* of "substantially limiting impairment" is still protected under the ADA. This provision was put in place to protect people with a history of such things as cancer, heart disease, mental illness, and the like from discrimination because of prior conditions, even if they are now in good health.

Those who are "regarded as having a disability" are protected as though they had an actual disability under the ADA. This situation would arise if an employer's attitude toward a condition was such that he or she perceived it as a disability. For instance, if a person had severe scars from a facial burn, and an employer felt there would be adverse reactions to this person, there is a "regarded disability." Another scenario would be if unfounded rumors started within a company that a person had a condition (HIV, for instance) and then that person was discriminated against. The person was perceived as having a disability, even though it was entirely untrue, and is therefore protected by the ADA. However, if a person regards him- or herself as having a disability, but in fact does not have one and is not treated as though he or she does, this person is not protected.

Now let's go back to the original definition. The law says you cannot discriminate against a *qualified* individual with a disability. That does not mean people with disabilities can apply for any job they think would be nice to have!

Qualified means the individual has the required skill, experience, education, licensing, and other job-related requirements for the position and can perform the essential functions of the job. The essential functions of a job are those that the person was hired to do or are performed on a routine basis as a primary part of the job. For instance, if a person was hired to operate a telephone switchboard but occasionally had to type a memo, typing is not an essential function of the job. Otherwise qualified takes into account the various other requirements an employer may place on individuals. For example, if an employer requires all employees to be fingerprinted, a person with a disability who has the necessary qualifications to do the job, but refuses to be fingerprinted, is not otherwise qualified to do the job.

The law in no way imposes on employers the burden of hiring unqualified workers, and it is not an affirmative action law that requires a percentage of the workforce to be disabled workers. It was written for the sole purpose of assuring that people who need a reasonable accommodation in the workplace in order to be able to compete for jobs, on an equal basis with nondisabled people, get that chance.

In order to determine if a person is qualified to perform the essential functions of a job, it is necessary to identify those functions precisely.

It is vital for an employer to list the essential functions of a job before interviewing applicants. Employers should look at each position and apply certain criteria to the various functions to determine if they are, indeed, essential. If a person is hired solely for an ability to perform a certain function, it is obviously essential. A function is essential if the number of other employees available to do the job is limited and asking them to absorb additional tasks is an undue hardship.

The amount of time an employee spends actually doing the job is an indication of whether it is essential. When a person does a particular thing for a predominant part of the workday, it is essential. The functions done for the remainder of the time may or may not be also essential to the job. However, if the function in question is only performed for a brief time, but is critical to the entire job, it is also essential. The amount of time a pilot spends landing the plane is short compared to the time in the air, but the ability to land the plane safely is critical to the job.

Deciding if a function is essential is done on a case-by-case basis. But it is important to look at what the job is to accomplish and not confuse that with how it is done. For example, if a job requires that fifty-pound boxes be moved from the loading dock to the storeroom, it may not be important that the applicant be able to lift the boxes, but only that they get moved in some way.

When employers determine the essential functions of a job, they may be required to show that they actually require those functions of people presently employed in the same position. If a new secretary position requires typing seventy-five words per minute, then other secretaries in the company must meet the same standard.

Contrary to popular opinion, the ADA does not require employers to develop or maintain job descriptions. But a well-written job description, listing essential and auxilliary functions, prepared before screening applicants, will be considered evidence of the essential functions of a job in the event of a complaint.

Qualified individuals with disabilities are protected from discrimination in all aspects of the employment process. This includes job application procedures, hiring, advancement or discharge, employee compensation, job training, and all other terms, conditions, and privileges of employment. Therefore, it is essential to understand what constitutes discrimination.

1. *Not making reasonable accommodation.* Employers must make a reasonable accommodation to the known limitations of a qualified person with a disability who is either an applicant or a current employee. If the accommodation imposes an additional burden on the person instead of helping, it is not an accommodation that provides the person with an equal meaningful employment opportunity, and it is discriminatory.

When a person with a disability who needs accommodation is otherwise equally qualified as a person without a disability, an employer cannot reject the person with a disability if the reason for the rejection is the reasonable accommodation requirement, except in such cases where the employer can prove the accommodation would present an undue hardship.

2. *Unfair standards or administrative methods.* Discrimination includes using standards or administrative methods that have the effect of discriminating. The employer should evaluate employment standards to be sure they include only the essential functions of the job, if they tend to exclude a person with a disability.

3. *Qualification standards and employment tests.* Testing, qualifying standards, or other selection criteria must be unbiased, including selection criteria for safety requirements, vision or hearing requirements, walking requirements, lifting requirements, and employment testing.

People are not to be excluded from jobs that they can actually perform merely because a disability prevents them from taking a test or negatively influences the results of a test. This requirement is in effect only when the employer knows prior to the test that the employee needs accommodation for the test taking.

If a person needs a test in large print or braille, or via a reader or sign interpreter, the employer may be required to provide the test in the requested form or in another form that will not reflect the area of disability.

Employment tests that require the use of sensory, manual, or speaking skills in order to measure those skills specifically are not unlawful as long as the skill being tested is an essential function of the job. For example, if you are hiring an ice cream taste tester, you can require a person to be able to taste the difference between chocolate and vanilla.

4. *Limiting, segregating, or classifying because of disabilities.* Employers must make employment decisions based on an individual's ability to do the job, not on assumptions of what a class of individuals with disabilities can or cannot do. An employer cannot limit or classify a person in such a way that negatively affects that person's employment status. Employers cannot segregate employees with disabilities into separate work areas or into separate lines of advancement. This would include such things as opportunities for business travel, attendance at conventions, or interacting with customers if other persons in the same job category are offered these opportunities.

Employers are not required to make accommodations that would result in undue hardship for the company. Undue hardship means a significant difficulty or expense involved with providing an accommodation. Undue hardship can also mean any accommodation that would be disruptive or that would fundamentally change the nature or operation of the business. For example, an ice cream maker who is intolerant of cold because of a recognized disability cannot ask that the freezers be turned off, because that would fundamentally change the nature of the ice cream.

If undue hardship is cited as the reason for failing to provide accommodation, the employer will have to prove the hardship. In most cases it will be difficult to prove based on financial measures alone. However, hardship based on disruption of the nature of the business will be somewhat easier to defend.

Employers cannot prove undue hardship if the disruption was the result of the fears or prejudices of the current employees toward a person's disability. Disruption can only be based on the provision of the accommodation.

When an employer is financially unable to provide an accommodation, the employer can still be required to provide accommodation if the funding is available from other sources. The funding can come from such sources as state vocational rehabilitation agencies; federal, state, or local tax deductions; or tax credits. The person with the disability can be a source of funding as well.

The Omnibus Budget Reconciliation Act of 1990 creates a "disabled access" tax credit for small businesses equal to 50 percent of expenses in excess of $250 to $10,250. The maximum credit, therefore, is $5,000 ($10,250 − $250 = $10,000 × 50% = $5,000). A small business eligible for help must meet either of two guidelines: (1) gross receipts for the preceding year that did not exceed $1 million, or (2) employed no more than thirty full-time employees during the preceding tax year.

Expenditures that are eligible for tax credit for the purpose of complying with the ADA are those reasonable and necessary amounts paid or incurred: (1) for the purpose of removing architectural, communication, physical, or transportation barriers that prevent a business from being accessible to, or usable by, disabled individuals; (2) to provide qualified interpreters or other effective methods of making aurally delivered materials available to hearing-impaired individuals; (3) to provide qualified readers, taped tests, and other effective methods of making visually delivered materials available to visually impaired individuals; (4) to acquire or modify equipment or devices for disabled individuals; or (5) to provide other similar services, modifications, materials, or equipment. Accessibility features in new construction are not eligible for the credit, nor are costs incurred in modifying a facility built after November 5, 1990.

Medical information relating to employment has become an area of concern for many employers. Employers may ask potential employees if they have the ability to perform job-related activities as long as the questions are not asked in terms of disability. If the person has a visible disability, the employer can ask, "How will you perform this job?" The employer may not ask, "Do you have a disability (limitation, medical condition, etc.) that would prevent you from doing this job?"

If the employer chooses to ask how a potential employee will perform a job, the employer must be willing to provide the reasonable accommodation the applicant needs to demonstrate the skill or accept an explanation of how that person will do the job when the accommodation is available.

Any attempt to identify a disability by inquiry or examination at the preoffer stage of the employment process is prohibited. However, after an offer of employment has been made, an employer can require a medical examination, and actual employment can be conditional on the results of the examination but only if all new employees in the same job category are required to take the same examination.

Information obtained during a medical examination must be kept strictly confidential and separate from general personnel files, with three important exceptions:

1. When supervisors or managers may need to be informed regarding necessary restrictions on the work or responsibilities of the employee
2. When the disability might require emergency treatment (first aid and safety personnel should be carefully trained in the care required)
3. When government officials investigating compliance with the ADA request the information

The results of the medical examination cannot be used to discriminate against a person with a disability if the person is otherwise qualified for the job. When disqualifying a person on the basis of the examination there are three points to consider:

1. If the disqualification is based on the probability of substantial harm, there must be valid medical data to substantiate this decision.
2. Any decision by the company's physician can be challenged by the applicant's physician.
3. Employment decisions cannot be based on a misguided attempt to protect the applicant from a perceived harm.

The ADA does not override any medical standards that have been established by federal, state, or local law as a prerequisite for performing a particular job. For example, pilots may have to meet certain medical standards for the sake of public safety. Legitimate medical reasons for denying employment are valid but must be provable!

Appendix C: Facility Compliance Check List

The following pages contain an Americans with Disabilities Act Compliance Check List, used by a group of hospitals to determine the physical accessibility of their facilities. This list may need to be customized for different building types and uses, but gives a good example of what to look for when checking accessibility.

Remember, wheelchairs are not the only concern. People who are blind or sight-impaired, and people who are deaf or hearing-impaired, need equal access, too!

SELF INSPECTION   CHECK LIST

Priority 1:	YES	NO	Possible Solutions
Accessible Entrance			
Is there a path of travel that does not require the use of stairs?			1. Add a ramp if the path of travel is interrupted by stairs. 2. Add an alternative pathway on level ground.
Is the path of travel stable, firm and slip-resistant?			1. Repair uneven paving 2. Fill small bumps and breaks with beveled patches 3. Replace gravel with hard top
Is the path at least 36 inches wide?			1. Change or move landscaping, furnishings or other features that narrow the path of travel 2. Widen the pathway
Can all objects protruding into the path be detected by a person with a visual disability using a cane?			1. Move or remove protruding objects 2. Add a cane-detectable base that extends to the ground.
Do curbs on the pathway have curbs cuts at drives, parking, and drop-offs?			1. Install curb cut 2. Add small ramp up to curb
Are the slopes of ramps no greater than 1:12? (See note 2)			1. Lengthen ramp to decrease slope 2. Relocate ramp 3. If space is limited, use switchbacks
Do all ramps longer than 6 feet have railings on both sides?			1. Add railings
Are railing sturdy, and between 34 and 38 inches high?			1. Adjust height of railings 2. Secure handrails
Is the width between railings at least 36 inches?			1. Relocate the railings 2. Widen the ramp
Are ramps non-slip?			1. Add non-slip surface material
Is there a 5' level landing at every 30' run of ramp (including top and bottom)			1. Remodel or relocate ramp
Are an adequate number of accessible parking spaces available? (See note 3)			1. Reconfigure a reasonable number of spaces by repainting stripes
Are 16-foot wide spaces, with 98 inches of vertical clearance, available for lift-equipped vans? (See note 4)			1. Reconfigure to provide a reasonable number of van accessible spaces.
Are the accessible spaces closest to the accessible entrance?			1. Reconfigure spaces

Are accessible spaces marked with the International Symbol of Accessibility?		1. Add signs, placed so that they are not obstructed by cars
Are there signs reading "Van Accessible" at van spaces?		1. Add signs
Is there an enforcement procedure to ensure that accessible parking is used only by those who need it?		1. Implement a policy to check periodically for violators and report them to the proper authorities
If there are stairs at the main entrance, is there also a ramp or lift, or is there an alternative accessible entrance? (See note 5)		If main entrance is inaccessible, create a dignified alternate accessible entrance. Make sure there is accessible parking near accessible entrances.
Do all inaccessible entrances have signs indicating the location of the nearest accessible entrance?		1. Install signs at or before inaccessible entrances.
Can the alternate accessible entrance be used independently?		1. Eliminate as much as possible the need for assistance
Does the entrance door have at least 32 inches clear opening (for a double door, at least one 32" leaf)?		1. Widen the door 2. Install offset (swing-clear) hinges
Is there at least 18 inches of clear wall space on the pull side of the door next to the handle? (See Note 6)		1. Remove or relocate furnishings, partitions, or other obstructions 2. Move door 3. Add power-assisted door opener
Is the threshold level (less than 1/4") or beveled, up to 1/2 " high?		1. If there is a single step with a rise of 6" or less, add a short ramp 2. If there is a high threshold, remove it or add a bevel
Are doormats 1/2" high or less and secured to the floor at all edges?		1. Replace or remove mats 2. Secure mats at edges
Is the door handle no higher than 48 inches and operable with a closed fist? (See Note 7)		1. Replace inaccessible knob with a lever or loop handle 2. Retrofit with an add-on lever extension
Can doors be opened without too much force (5 pounds maximum)?		1. Adjust the door closers and oil the hinges 2. Install power-assisted door openers
If the door has a closer, does it take at least 3 seconds to close?		1. Adjust door closer
Do all alarms for emergency egress have both flashing lights and audible signals?		1. Install visible and audible alarms
Is there sufficient lighting in egress pathways such as stairs, corridors, and exits?		1. Upgrade, add, or clean bulbs or fixtures

PRIORITY 2:			
ACCESS TO GOODS AND SERVICES			
Does the accessible entrance provide direct access to the main floor, lobby, or elevator?			1. Add ramps or lifts 2. Make another entrance accessible
Are all public spaces on an accessible path of travel?			1. Provide access to all public spaces along an accessible path of travel.
Is the accessible route to all public spaces at least 36 inches wide?			1. Move furnishings such as tables, chairs, display racks, vending machines, and counters to make more room.
Is there a 5' circle or a T-shaped space for a person using a wheelchair to reverse direction?			Rearrange furnishings, displays, and equipment
Do doors into public spaces have at least a 32 inch clear opening?			1. Install offset (swing-clear) hinges. 2. Widen doors
On the pull side of doors, next to the handle, is there at least 18' of clear wall space so that a person using a wheelchair can get near the door?			1. Reverse the door swing if it is safe to do so 2. Move or remove obstructing partitions
Can doors be opened without too much force (5 pounds maximum)?			1. Adjust or replace closers 2. Install lighter doors 3. Install power-assisted door openers
Are door handles 48 inches high or less and operable with a closed fist?			1. Lower handles 2. Replace inaccessible hardware with lever or loop handles 3. Install power-assisted door opener
Are all thresholds level (less than 1/4"), or beveled, up to 1/2" high?			1. Remove thresholds 2. Add bevels to both sides
Are all aisles and pathways to all goods and services at least 36 inches wide?			1. Rearrange furnishings and fixtures to clear aisles
Is there a 5-foot circle or T-shaped space for turning a wheelchair completely?			1. Rearrange furnishings to clear more room
Is carpeting low-pile, tightly woven, and securely attached along edges?			1. Secure edges on all sides 2. Replace carpeting
Are all obstacles cane-detectable (Located within 27" of the floor) or protruding less than 4" from the wall, or higher than 80" in routes through public areas			1. Remove obstacles 2. Install furnishings, planters, or other cane-detectable barriers underneath the obstacle
Do signs designating permanent rooms and spaces, such as rest room signs, exit signs, and room numbers, comply with the appropriate requirements for accessible signage? (See Note 8)			1. Provide signage that has raised and brailled letters, complies with finish and contrast standards, and is mounted at the correct height and location

Question			Solution
Are all controls that are available for use by the public(game and self-service, etc.) located at an accessible height?			1. Relocate controls
Are they operable with a closed fist?			1. Replace controls
Are the aisles between chairs, tables and counters at least 36 inches wide? (See Note 9)			1. Rearrange chairs or tables
Are the spaces for wheelchair seating distributed throughout?			1. Rearrange tables to allow room for wheelchairs 2. Remove some fixed seating
Are the tops of tables or counters between 28 and 34 inches high?			1. Lower at least a section of high tables and counters
Are knee spaces at accessible tables at least 27 inches high, 30 inches wide, and 19 inches deep?			1. Replace or raise tables
Are there ramps or elevators to all levels?			1. Install ramps or lifts 2. Modify an elevator 3. Relocate goods or services to an accessible area
On each level, if there are stairs between the entrance and/or elevator and essential public areas, is there an accessible alternate route?			1. Post clear signs directing people along an accessible route to ramps, lifts, or elevators
Do stair treads have a non-slip surface?			1. Add non-slip surface to treads
Do stairs have continuous rails on both sides, with extensions beyond the top and bottom stairs?			1. Add or replace handrails
Are there both visible, verbal or audible door opening/closing and floor indicators?			1. Install visible and verbal or audible signals
Are the elevator call buttons in the hallway no higher than 42 inches?			1. Lower call buttons 2. Provide a permanently attached reach stick
Do the controls outside and inside the cab have raised and braille lettering?			1. Install raised lettering and braille next to buttons
Is there a sign on the jamb at each floor identifying the floor in raised and braille letters?			1. Install tactile signs to identify floor numbers, at a height of 60 inches from floor
Is the emergency intercom usable without voice communication?			1. Replace communication system
Are there braille and raised-letter instructions for the communication system?			1. Add simple tactile instructions

Can the wheelchair lift be used without assistance? If not is a call button provided?			1. Post clear instructions for use of the lift 2. Provide a call button
Is there at least 30 by 48 inches of clear space for a person using a wheelchair to approach to reach the controls and use the lift?			1. Rearrange furnishings and equipment to clear more space
Are controls between 15 and 48 inches high? (Up to 54 inches if a side approach is possible)			1. Move controls
PRIORITY 3:			
USABILITY OF REST ROOMS			
If rest rooms are available to the public, is at least one rest room (either one for each sex, or unisex) fully accessible?			1. Reconfigure rest room 2. Combine rest rooms to create one unisex accessible rest room
Are there signs at inaccessible rest rooms that give directions to accessible ones?			1. Install signs
Is there tactile signage identifying rest rooms? (See Note 10)			1. Add accessible signage, placed to the side of the door 2. If symbols are used, add verbal signage
Is the doorway at least 32 inches clear?			1. Install offset (swing-clear) hinges 2. Widen doorway
Are doors equipped with accessible handles (operable with a closed fist), 48 inches high or less?			1. Lower handles 2. Replace inaccessible knobs or latches 3. Add lever extensions
Can doors be opened easily (5 pounds maximum force)			1. Install lighter doors
Does the entry configuration provide adequate maneuvering space for a person using a wheelchair? (See Note 11)			1. Rearrange furnishings such as chairs and trash cans. 2. Remove inner door if there is a vestibule 3. Move or remove obstructing partitions.
Is there a 36' wide path to all fixtures?			1. Remove obstructions
Is the stall door operable with a closed fist, inside and out?			1. Replace inaccessible knobs with lever or loop handles 2. Add lever extensions
Is there a wheelchair-accessible stall that has an area of at least 5' by 5', clear of the door swing, OR a stall that provides either 36" by 69" or 48" by 69"?			1. Move or remove partitions 2. Reverse the door swing if it is safe to do so

In the accessible stall, are there grab bars behind and on the side wall nearest to the toilet?		1. Add grab bars
Is the toilet seat 17 to 19 inches high?		1. Add raised seat
Does one lavatory have a 30" wide by 48" deep clear space in front? (See Note 12)		1. Rearrange furnishings 2. Replace lavatory 3. Remove or alter cabinetry
Is the lavatory rim no higher than 34 inches?		1. Adjust or replace lavatory
Is there at least 29 inches from the floor to the bottom of the lavatory apron (excluding pipes)?		1. Adjust or replace lavatory
Can the faucet be operated with one closed fist?		1. Replace faucet handles with paddle type
Are soap and other dispensers and hand dryers 48 inches high or less and usable with one closed fist?		1. Lower dispensers 2. Replace with or provide additional accessible dispensers
Is the mirror mounted with the bottom edge of the reflecting surface 40 inches high or lower?		1. Lower or tilt down the mirror 2. Replace with larger mirror
PRIORITY 4:		
ADDITIONAL ACCESS		
Is there at least one drinking fountain with clear floor space of at least 30 by 48 inches in front?		1. Clear more room by rearranging or removing furnishings.
Is there one fountain with its spout no higher than 36" from the ground, and another with a standard height spout (or a single "hi-lo" fountain?		1. Provide cup dispensers for fountains with spouts that are too high 2. Provide an accessible water cooler
Are controls mounted on the front or on the side near the front edge and operable with one closed fist?		1. Replace the controls
Does the fountain protrude no more than 4 inches into the circulation space?		1. Place a planter or other cane-detectable barrier on each side at floor level
Do pay or public use phones have a clear floor space of at least 30 by 48 inches in front of at least one?		1. Move furnishings 2. Replace booth with open stations
Is the highest operable part of the phone no higher than 48 inches (up to 54" if side approach is possible)?		1. Lower telephone

Does the phone protrude no more than 4 inches into the circulation area?			1. Place a cane-detectable barrier on each side at floor level
Does the phone have push-button controls?			1. Contact phone company to install push-buttons
Is the phone hearing aid compatible?			1. Contact phone company to add an induction coil
Is the phone adapted with volume control?			1. Contact the phone company to add volume control
Is the phone with volume control identified with appropriate signage?			1. Add signage
Is one of the phone equipped with text telephone (TT or TD)?			1. Install a text telephone 2. Have a portable text telephone available
Is the location of the text telephone identified by accessible signage bearing the International TDD Symbol?			1. Add signage

Note #1	In order to be detected using a cane, an object must be within 27" of the ground. Objects hanging or mounted overhead must be higher than 80 inches to provide clear head room. It is not necessary to remove objects that protrude less than 4" from walls
Note #2	Slope of 1:12 means for every 12" along the base of the ramp, the height increases one inch. For a 1:12 maximum slope, at least one foot of ramp length is needed for each inch of height.
Note #3	An accessible space is 8 feet wide for car plus 5-foot striped access aisle. For guidance in determining the appropriate number of spaces, see chart below
Note #4	At least one of every eight accessible spaces must be van accessible
Note #5	Do not use a service entrance as the accessible entrance unless there is NO other option
Note #6	A person using a wheelchair needs this space to get close enough to open the door
Note #7	The 'closed fist' test for handles and controls: Try opening the door or operating the control using only one hand, held in a fist. If you can do it, so can a person who has limited use of his or her hands.
Note #8	Character and background must contrast and be eggshell, matte or non-glare finish. Mount on wall on latch side of doors, 60" above floor
Note #8A	Person must be able to approach within 3" of sign without encountering protruding objects or standing within the swing of a door
Note #9	The maximum height for a side reach is 54 inches, for a forward reach, 48 inches. The minimum reachable height is 15 inches
Note #10	Avoid using ambiguous symbols in place of text to identify rest rooms
Note #11	A person in a wheelchair needs 36" of clear width for forward movement and a 5' diameter clear space or a T-shaped space to make turns. A minimum distance of 48", clear of doors, is needed between the 2 doors of an entry vestibule
Note #12	A maximum of 19" of the required depth may be under the lavatory. Make sure hot pipes are insulated.

TOTAL SPACES AVAILABLE	MINIMUM ACCESSIBLE SPACES
1 TO 25	1
26 TO 50	2
51 TO 75	3
76 TO 100	4
101 TO 150	5
151 TO 200	6
201 TO 300	7
301 TO 400	8
401 TO 500	9
501 TO 1000	2% OF TOTAL

One in every eight accessible spaces must be designed for use by a van deploying a wheelchair lift. This means the access aisle must be a minimum of ninety-six inches wide. Access aisles for ordinary accessible spaces must have an access aisle sixty inches wide.

Glossary

ACUTE: of short or sudden course; sharp

ALVEOLI: air cells in the lung

AMELIA: absence of a limb or limbs

AMPUTATION, ACQUIRED: removal of a limb or appendage through surgery or accident

AMPUTATION, CONGENITAL: the failure of a limb or appendage to develop in a fetus; the absence of a whole or a part of a limb at birth

ANEURYSM: a weakened area on an artery which becomes dilated with blood

ANGIOPLASTY: reconstruction or repair of an injured blood vessel

ANOXIA: an absence of oxygen

ANTERIOR: in front of, or toward the head end of

ANTIBODY: a substance in the blood developed to neutralize an unwanted organism and to provide immunity to that organism

AORTA: the main trunk of the arterial system, arising from the left ventricle and distributing aterial blood to all parts of the body

APHASIA: loss or impairment of the ability to use words as symbols of ideas

ARTERY: a blood vessel carrying blood away from the heart

ARTHROGRYPOSIS: a congenital disease manifested by stiff and curved joints

ARTHROSCOPY: examination of the interior of a joint

ARTICULATION: the place of union or juncture between two bones

ASTHMA: a disease caused by spasmodic contraction of the bronchi, resulting in wheezing, coughing and respiratory difficulty

ASYMPTOMATIC: without apparent symptoms

ATAXIA: loss of the power to coordinate muscle movement

ATHETOSIS: constant succession of slow, involuntary movements

ATROPHY: a wasting away of tissues or organs

AURA: a sensation felt by a person just prior to a seizure

AXON: the only one of the processes surrounding a nerve cell capable of conducting an impulse away from the cell body

BENIGN: not involved in uncontrollable growth; passive

BRADYKINESIA: extreme slowness in movement

BULBAR: relating to the region of the brain which includes the pons, cerebellum and medulla oblongata

CARTILAGE: connective tissue characterized by lack of blood supply

CATHETER: a tube inserted into the organ, part of which remains outside the organ for various reasons

CEREBRAL PALSY: a disorder of movement and coordination caused by cerebral defect or injury

CHOREA: a disorder characterized by irregular, spasmodic involuntary movements of limbs or facial muscles

CHROMOSOMES: small rod-shaped or v-shaped bodies which appear in the nucleus of a cell during cell division and which contain the hereditary factors

CHRONIC: of long duration; continuous

CILIA: a hairlike structure capable of motion

CONGENITAL: existing at birth

CONTRACTURE: a permanent muscle contraction

CORNEA: the transparent fibrous sheath covering the iris and pupil in the eye

CYSTIC FIBROSIS: a hereditary disease of children involving defective production of enzymes in the pancreas, causing disturbances throughout the body and usually with pulmonary involvement

DEGENERATIVE: a change in tissue from a higher to a lower or less functionally active form

DEMENTIA: a general mental deterioration

DI: prefix denoting two, twice

DIABETES MELLITUS: a metabolic disorder of the pancreas resulting in faulty production of insulin leading to high blood sugar levels

DORSAL: pertaining to or situated on the back

DOWN SYNDROME: a congenital defect marked by chromosomal abnormality, mental retardation and some degree of physical deformity

DWARFISM: underdevelopment of part or all of the body due to malfunction of the endocrine glands or to disease

DYSLEXIA: impaired ability to read due to brain malfunction

DYSPLASIA: abnormal development or growth

DYSTROPHY: defective or faulty musculature

EMPHYSEMA: a swelling of the lungs due to the presence of trapped air or the dilation of the pulmonary alveoli or sacs, usually as the result of chronic inflammation

EPIDEMIOLOGY: study of prevalence and spread of disease in a community

EPILEPSY: a central nervous system disorder marked by transient periods of unconsciousness or psychic disturbance, twitching, delirium, or convulsive movements

EPITHELIUM: the purely cellular layer, having no blood supply, that covers all body tissue surfaces

FUSION: abnormal coherence of adjacent parts or bodies

GENETIC: having to do with heredity

GRAND MAL: a complete epileptic seizure, also called tonic-clonic seizure

HEMI: prefix denoting half

HEMIPLEGIA: paralysis of one side of the body

HEMOPHILIA: a serious hereditary disorder in which the blood fails to clot and in which deep tissue bleeding occurs following injury or bruising

HORMONE: a chemical substance secreted into the body by the endocrine glands, or by other secreting cells, which has a specific effect on the activity of a body organ

HYDROCEPHALUS: an abnormal condition in which there is excessive fluid in or around the brain

HYPER: prefix denoting excess

HYPERGLYCEMIA: abnormally high blood sugar

HYPO: prefix denoting deficiency

INFARCTION: sudden insufficiency of blood supply

INSULIN: a protein hormone produced by the pancreas which is essential to the metabolism of glucose

KYPHOSIS: backward curvature of the spine

LASER: a device that produces a beam of high-energy light

LATERAL: pertaining to the side

LESION: a wound or injury

LIGAMENT: fibrous tissue connecting two or more bones, cartilage, or other structures

LORDOSIS: an abnormally increased forward curvature of the lower spine

LUMBAR: pertaining to the lower back in the area of the kidneys

LYMPH: a clear fluid collected from tissues throughout the body and eventually added to the venous blood supply

MALAISE: a feeling of general discomfort or uneasiness

MALIGNANT: capable of uncontrollable growth

MEDIAL: pertaining to the middle

MENINGES: the three membranes enveloping the brain and spinal cord, namely the dura mater, the pia mater, and the arachnoid

MENINGITIS: inflammation of the membranes of the brain or spinal cord

MENINGOCELE: a protrusion of the meninges through a defect in the skull or a defect in the spinal column

METASTASIS: the shifting of a disease from one part of the body to another

MONGOLOID: see Down Syndrome

MUSCULAR DYSTROPHY: a hereditary disease, marked by progressive shrinking and wasting of skeletal muscle with no apparent lesion of the spinal cord

MYASTHENIA GRAVIS: fatigue and exhaustion of the muscular system without atrophy, but accompanied by progressive paralysis of certain muscles, especially those of the face, lips, tongue, throat, and neck

MYELIN: the material enveloping the axon of some nerve fibers

MYELOMENINGOCELE: protrusion of the spinal cord and its covering through an opening in the bony spinal canal

MYOCARDIAL: relating to the middle layer of the heart

NECROSIS: death of a tissue, usually as individual cells or groups of cells

NEUROFIBROMATOSIS: a hereditary disorder involving the development of tumors on the peripheral nerves, numbering into the hundreds, and distributed over the entire body

NEUROLOGICAL: having to do with the nervous system

NEURON: a unit of the nervous system consisting of the nerve cell body, axon, and dendrites

OCCUPATIONAL THERAPY: therapy in which the principal goal is productive or creative activity

OPTIC NERVE: either of a pair of cranial nerves conducting impulses from the retina to the brain

ORTHOTICS: the science or practice of straightening a deformed part with mechanical devices, e.g., braces

OSTEOGENESIS IMPERFECTA: a defect of bone formation characterized by bone fragility resulting in multiple fractures even before birth and in infancy

PARA: involvement of two like parts

PARESIS: incomplete paralysis

PARKINSON'S DISEASE: a progressive disease of later life involving tremor, masklike appearance, awkward gait, slowing of voluntary movements, and weakening of muscles

PATELLA: the kneecap

PERINATAL: before, during, or directly after birth

PETIT MAL: a mild convulsive disorder related to epilepsy characterized by sudden brief blackouts of consciousness followed by immediate recovery, also called absence seizures

PHOCOMELIA: a developmental abnormality in infants in which the hands or feet are attached directly to the trunk without the normal connective arm or leg bones

PHYSICAL THERAPY: the treatment of disease and injury by means such as exercise, heat, light, and massage

PLASMA: the fluid, noncellular portion of the circulating blood

PLASMAPHERESIS: a treatment which involves separating the blood corpuscles from the plasma, discarding the plasma, combining the corpuscles with new fluid, and returning the new combination to the patient

PLATELET: circular or oval disks in the blood which control the coagulation of the blood and the contraction of the clot

PLEGIA or PLEGIC: suffix meaning paralysis

POLIOMYELITIS: an acute viral disease which invades the nerve cells in the spinal cord or brain stem, resulting in paralysis or muscular atrophy. A mild form of the disease may involve only fever, sore throat, stiff neck, and headache

PROCESS: a projection or outgrowth

PROGNOSIS: a forecast as to the recovery or outcome of a condition based on the symptoms and current knowledge of the condition

PROSTHESIS: an artificial substitute for a missing part of the body

PROXIMAL: nearest to the point of reference

PSEUDO: false

PULMONARY: pertaining to the lungs

QUADRI: prefix denoting four

REMISSION: abatement or lessening of intensity in a disease, or the period during which such abatement occurs

RETINA: the light-receptive layer of the eye, continuous with the optic nerve, on which the image is produced

RHEUMATOID ARTHRITIS: a chronic disease characterized by inflammation of the joints, usually accompanied by marked deformities

SCOLIOSIS: sideward curvature of the spine

SENSORINEURAL LOSS: loss of sensation through the sensory nerves

SPASM: increased muscular tension that cannot be released voluntarily

SPINA BIFIDA: a congenital cleft in the bony encasement of the spinal cord, with meningeal protrusion

SPINAL CORD: that part of the central nervous system contained within the vertebral column

SYNDROME: a collection of signs and symptoms associated with a condition

SYNOVIAL: having to do with the fluid which lubricates a joint

THROMBOSIS: the development of a clot or plug in a blood vessel in the lungs or in the heart

TONIC-CLONIC: see Grand Mal

TRAUMA: accidental or inflicted wound

TREMOR: involuntary trembling or quivering in one or more parts of the body

VASCULAR: relating to or containing blood vessels

VEIN: a blood vessel carrying blood to the heart

For Further Reading

Bell, C. W. *Home Care and Rehabilitation in Respiratory Medicine*. Philadelphia, PA: J. B. Lippincott Co., 1984.

Bigge, E. and P. O'Donnell. *Teaching Individuals with Physical and Multiple Disabilities*, 2nd Ed. Columbus, OH: Charles E. Merrill, 1982.

Bishop, D., ed. *Behavioral Problems of the Disabled: Assessment and Management*. Baltimore, MD: Williams & Wilkins, 1980.

Bleck, E. and D. Nagel. *Physically Handicapped Children: A Medical Atlas for Teachers*, 2nd Ed. New York, NY: Grune & Stratton, 1982.

Business Law Editors. *Accommodating Disabilities: Business Management Guide*. Chicago, IL: Commerce Clearing House, Inc., 1992.

Cordellos, H. *Breaking Through*. Mountain View, CA: Anderson World, Inc., 1981.

Coventry, M. B., ed. *Yearbook of Orthopedics*. Chicago, IL: Year Book Medical Publications, 1984.

Davis, H. and R. Silverman. *Hearing and Deafness*. New York, NY: Holt, Rinehart & Winston, 1978.

Douglas, P. H. and L. Pinsky. *The Essential AIDS Fact Book*. New York, NY: Simon & Schuster, Inc., 1992.

Duvoisim, R. C. *Parkinson's Disease: A Guide for Patient and Family*, 3rd Ed. New York, NY: Raven Press, 1991.

Fleisher, L., L. Soodak, and M. Jelin. "Selective Attention Deficits in Learning Disabled Children," *Exceptional Children* 51, (2): 136–141.

Foley, C., and H. F. Pizer. *The Stroke Fact Book*. Golden Valley, MN: Courage Press, 1990.

Friedberg, E. C. *Cancer Answers*. New York, NY: W. H. Freeman & Co., 1992.

Greenblatt, M. H. *Multiple Sclerosis and Me*. Springfield, IL: Charles C. Thomas, 1972.

Grossman, H. J., ed., *Manual on Terminology and Classification in Mental Retardation*. Washington, DC: American Association on Mental Deficiency, 1984.

Kaplan, H. S., et al. *The Evaluation of Sexual Disorders: Psychological and Medical Aspects.* New York, NY: Brunner, Mazel, Inc., 1983.

Knoblock, P. *Teaching Emotionally Disturbed Children.* Hopewell, NJ: Houghton Mifflin, 1983.

McDaniel, J. W. *Physical Disability and Human Behavior.* New York, NY: Pergamon Press, 1976.

Radziunas, E. *Lupus, My Search for a Diagnosos.* Claremont, CA: Hunter House, Inc., 1989.

Rosner, L. J. and S. Ross. *Multiple Sclerosis.* New York, NY: Fireside, 1992.

Scheinberg, L. C. and N. J. Holland, eds. *Multiple Sclerosis: A Guide for Patients and Their Families*, 2nd Ed. New York, NY: Raven Press, 1987.

Thompson, G., I. Rubin, and R. Bilenker, eds. *Comprehensive Management of Cerebral Palsy.* New York, NY: Grune & Stratton, 1983.

Van Etten, A. M. "Dwarfs Don't Live in Doll Houses," *Accent on Living* 36 (Fall 1991): 110.

Williams, H . E., and P. D. Phelan. *Respiratory Illness in Children.* Oxford: Blackwell Scientific Publications, 1975.

Winnick, J. and F. Short. *Physical Fitness Testing of the Disabled: Project UNIQUE.* Champaign, IL: Human Kinetics Publishers, 1985.

Index

Page numbers in italic indicate main entries.

About the Author

DOROTHY STONELY SHROUT is co-founder of the National Instructors Association for Divers with Disabilities, an organization dedicated to making the aquatic world accessible to people who have a disability. She has traveled across the United States conducting classes and seminars on the medical and social aspects of disabilities. She assisted in developing a disabilities program at San Jose State University in California, has written extensively in the medical field, and is a member of the American Medical Writers Association (AMWA).